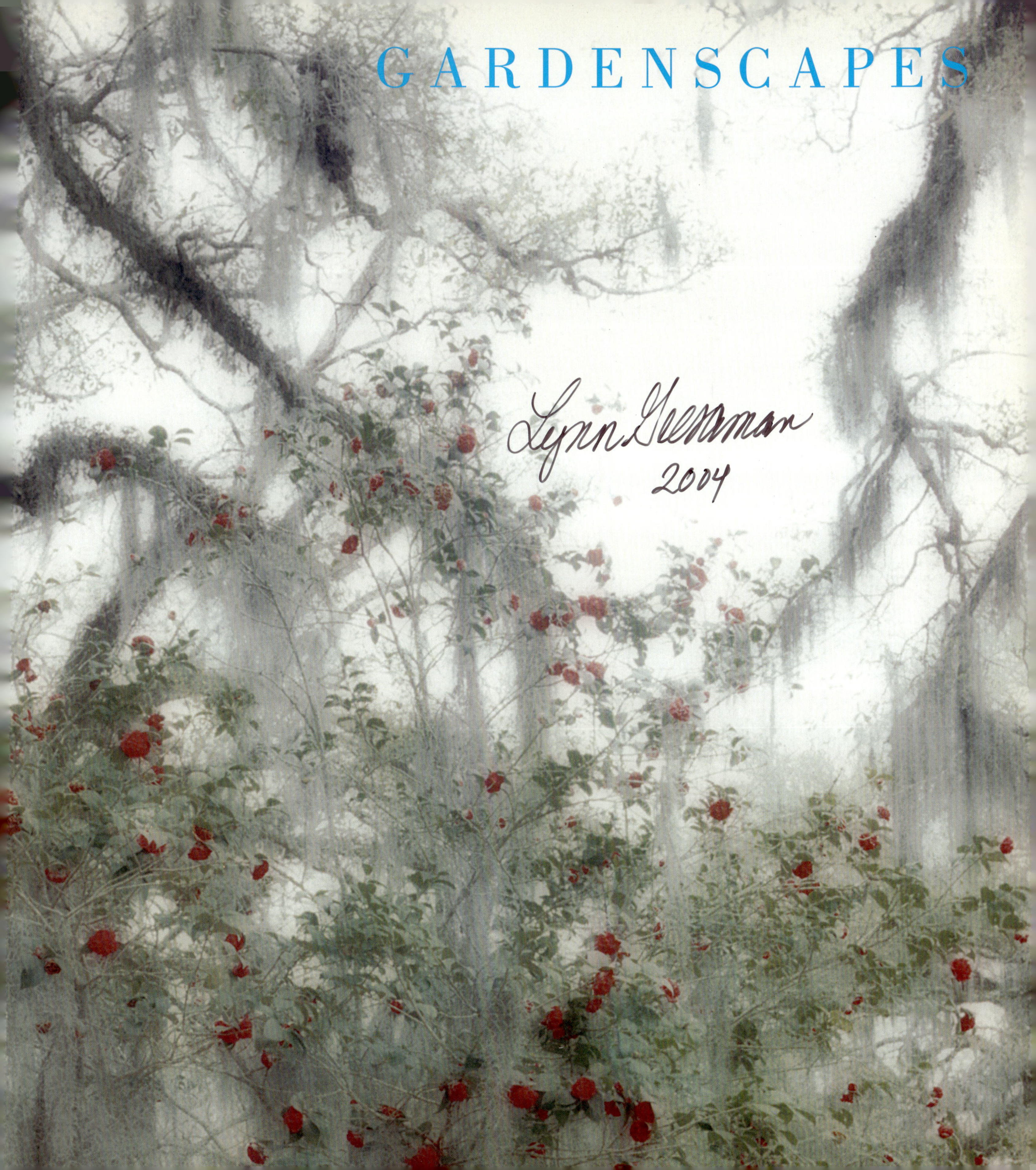
GARDENSCAPES
Lynn Geesaman
2004

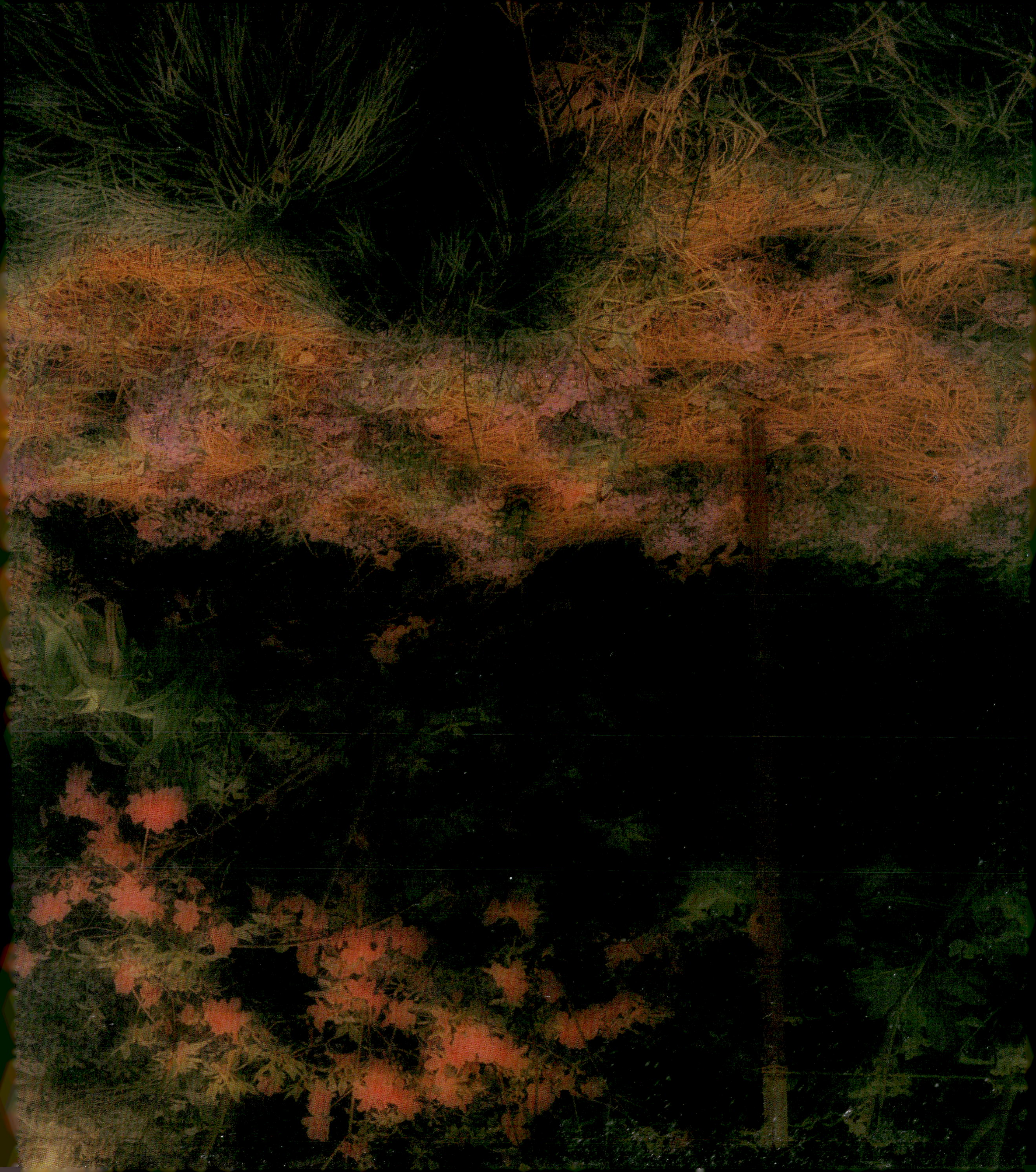

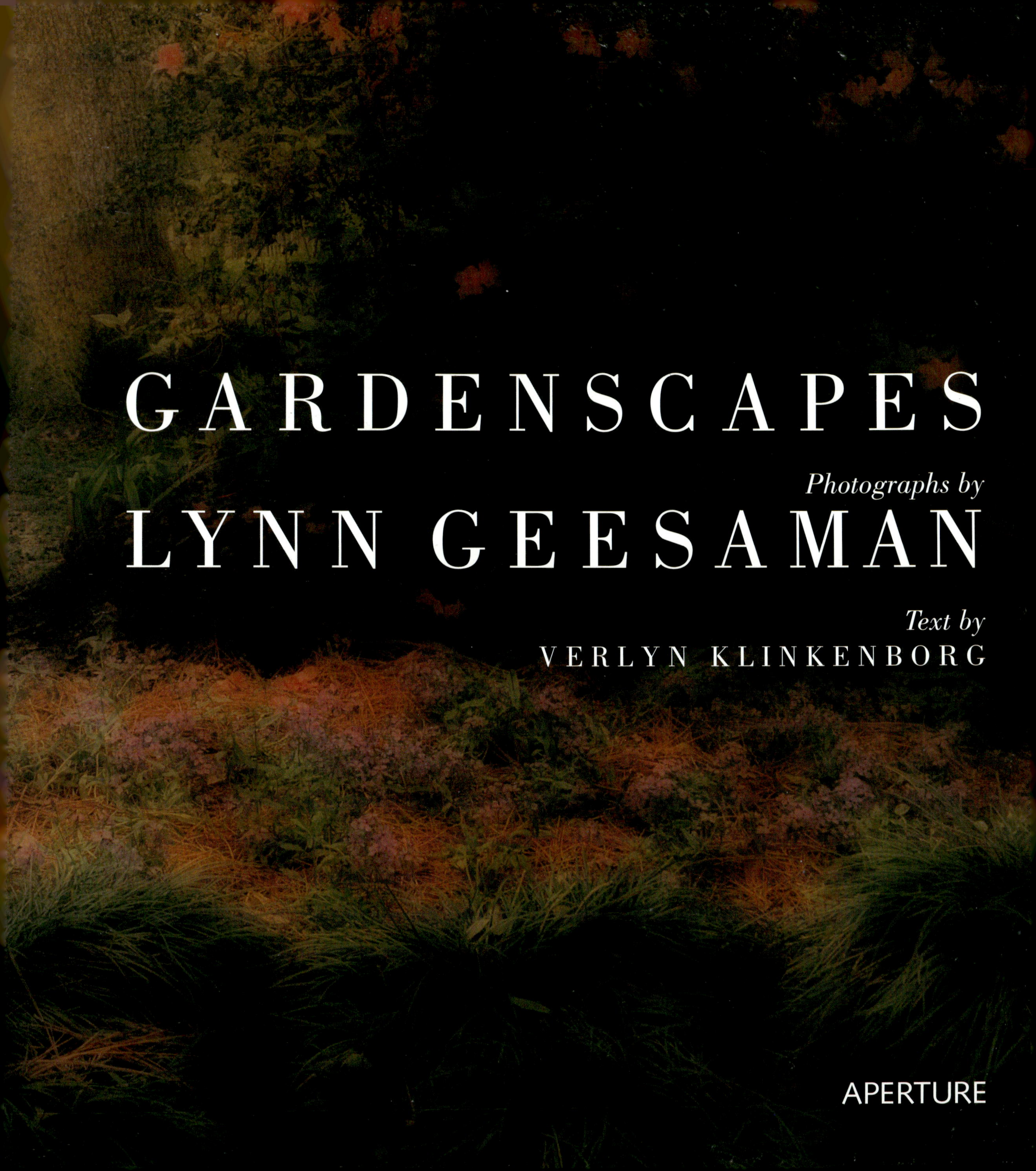

GARDENSCAPES

Photographs by
LYNN GEESAMAN

Text by
VERLYN KLINKENBORG

APERTURE

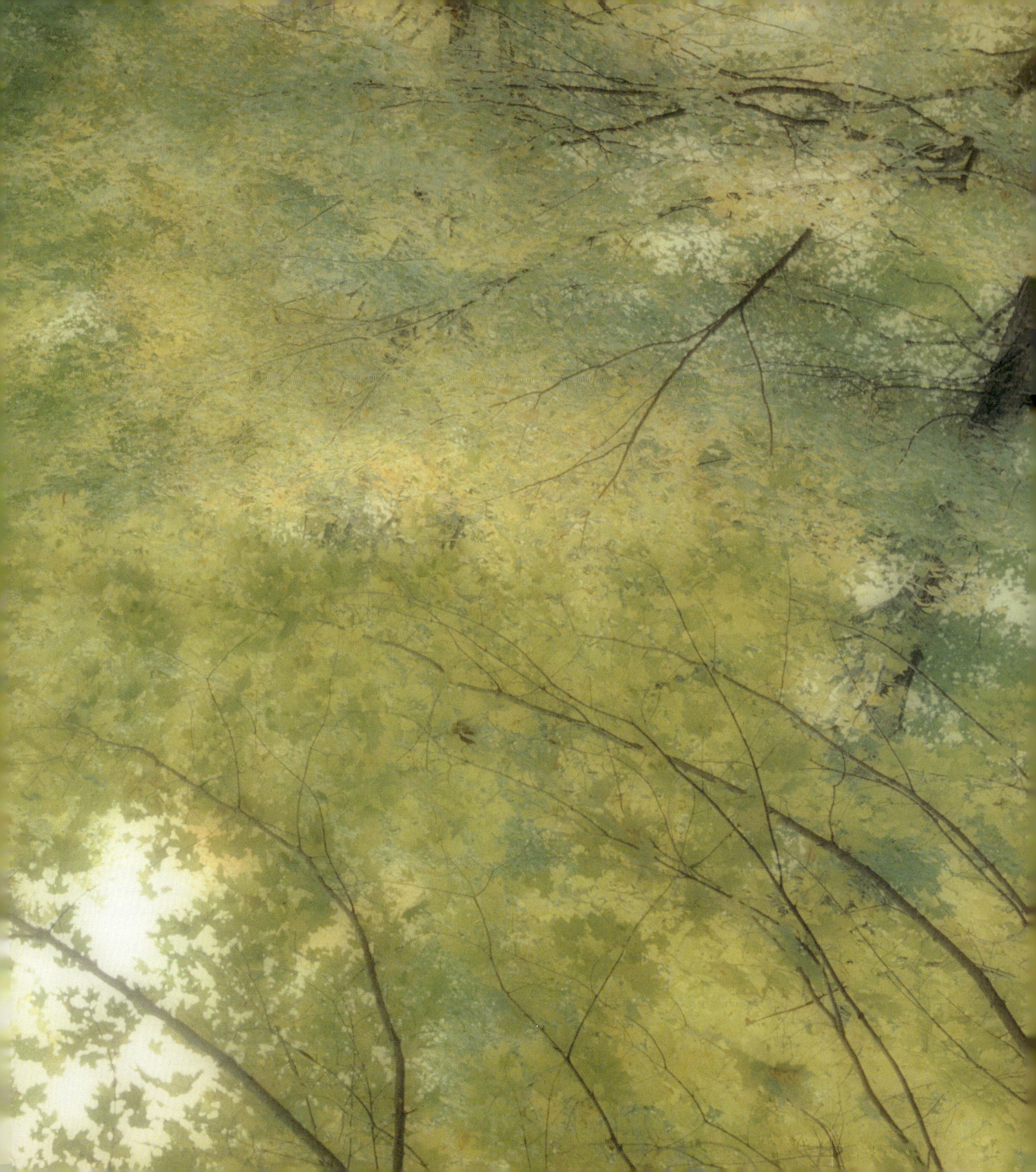

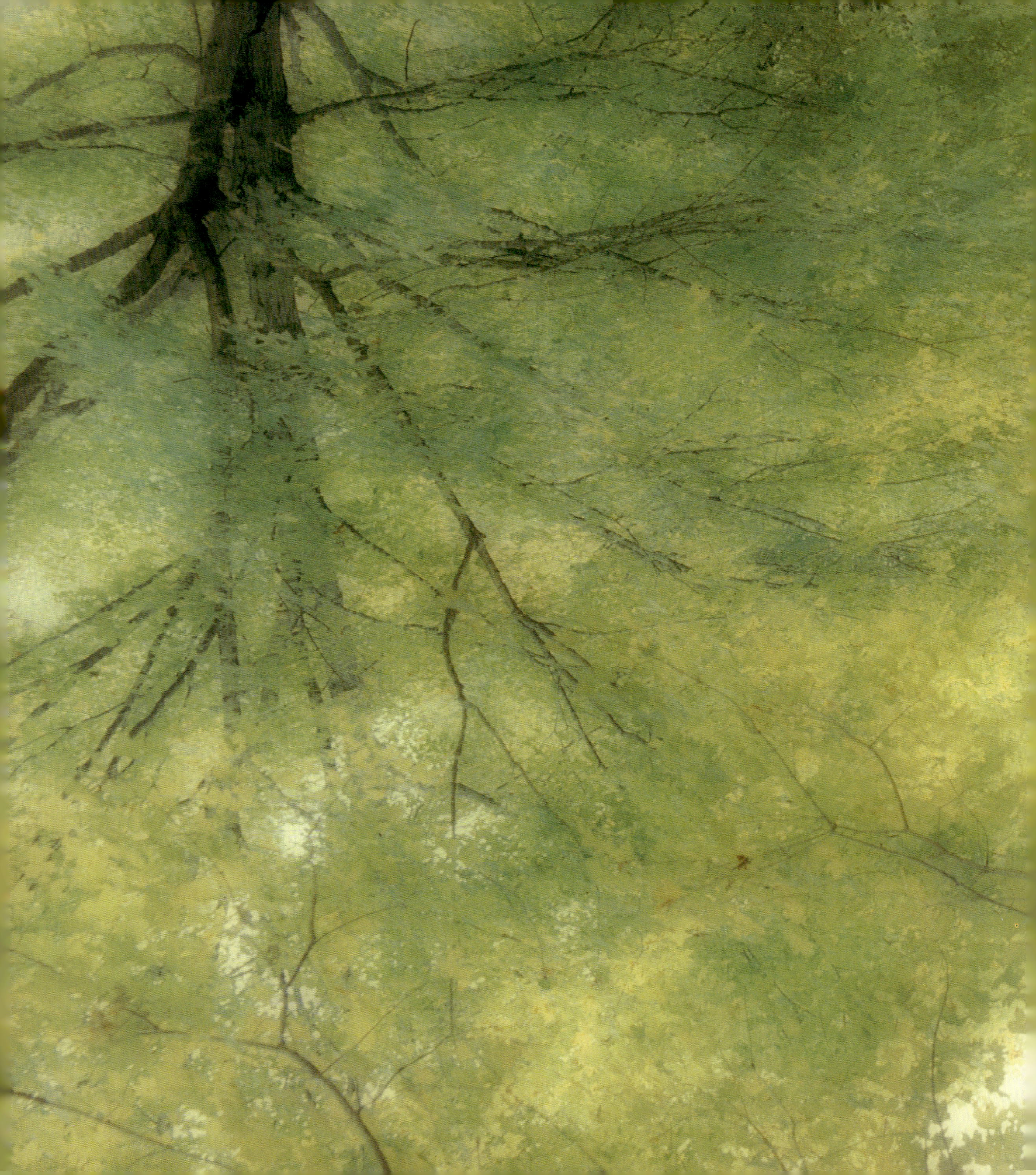

The photographs in this book span ten years and reflect a transition from black-and-white to color. Much of the work was made in Europe, where I continue to find black-and-white landscape subjects. With color, however, my range of subjects has expanded to include places that are less structured and more about color and light. Ultimately, despite all the planning and searching, it's just a matter of being in the right place at the right time.

—LYNN GEESAMAN

CONTENTS

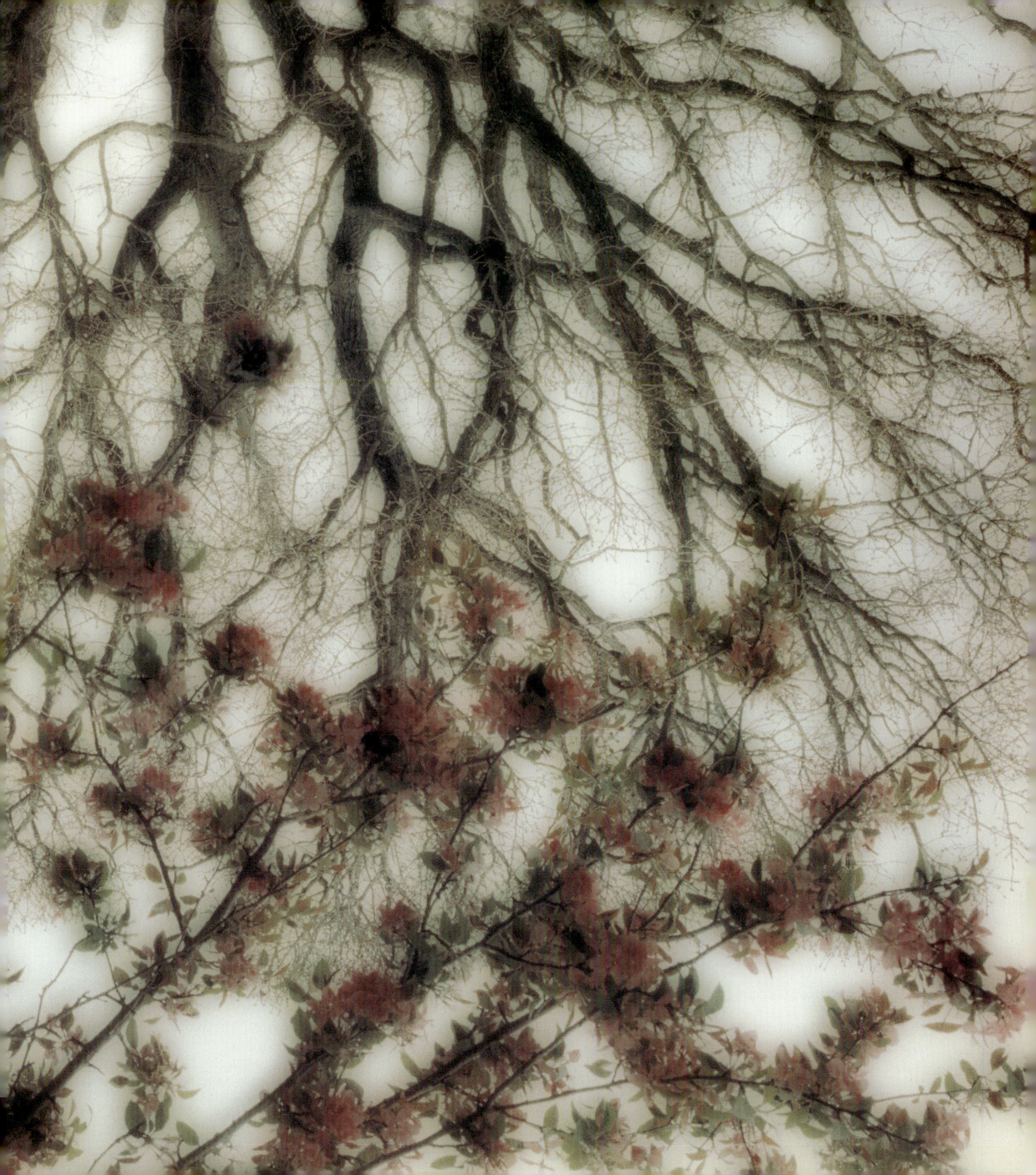

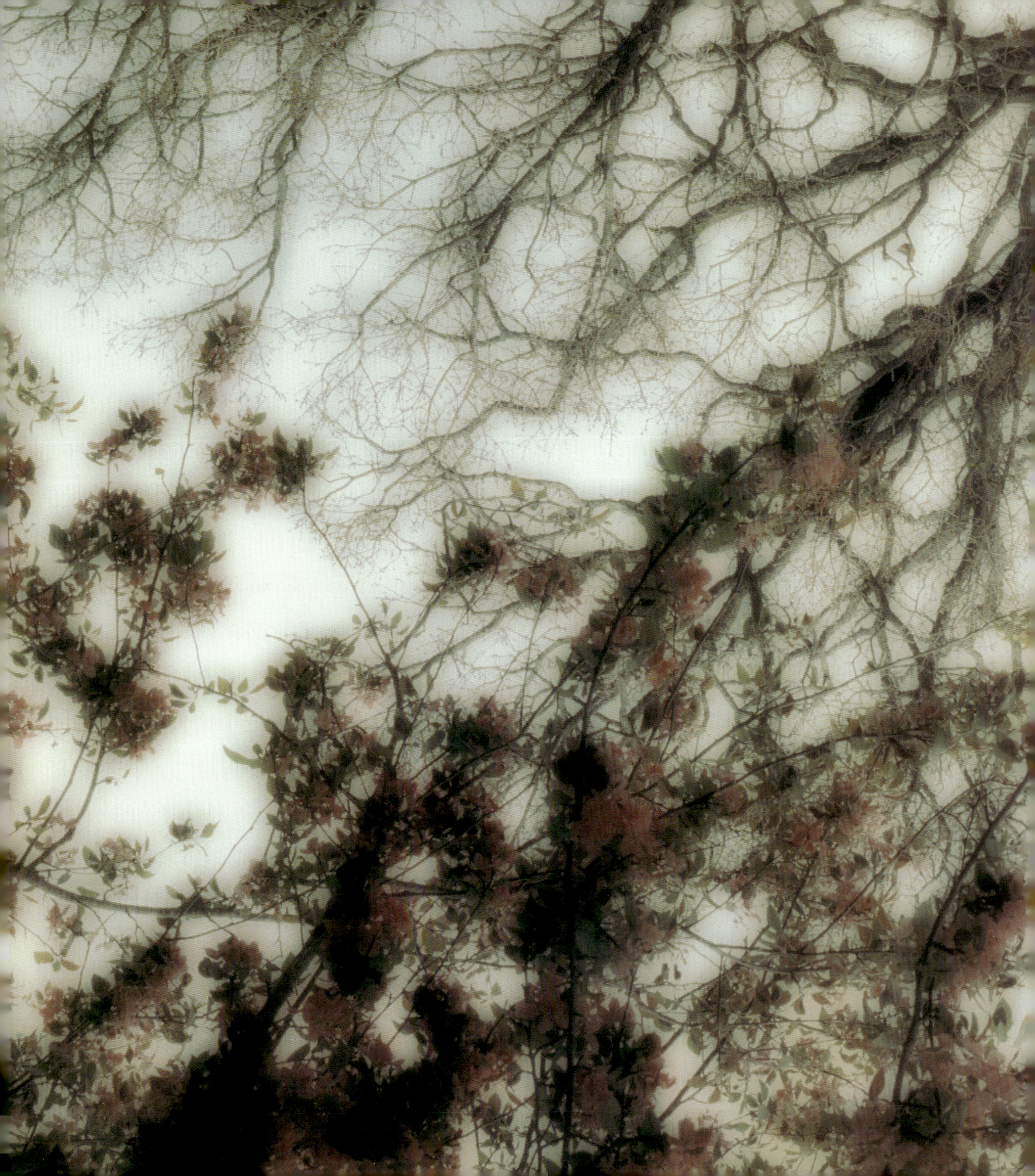

Waddesdon Manor, near Aylesbury, England, 1997

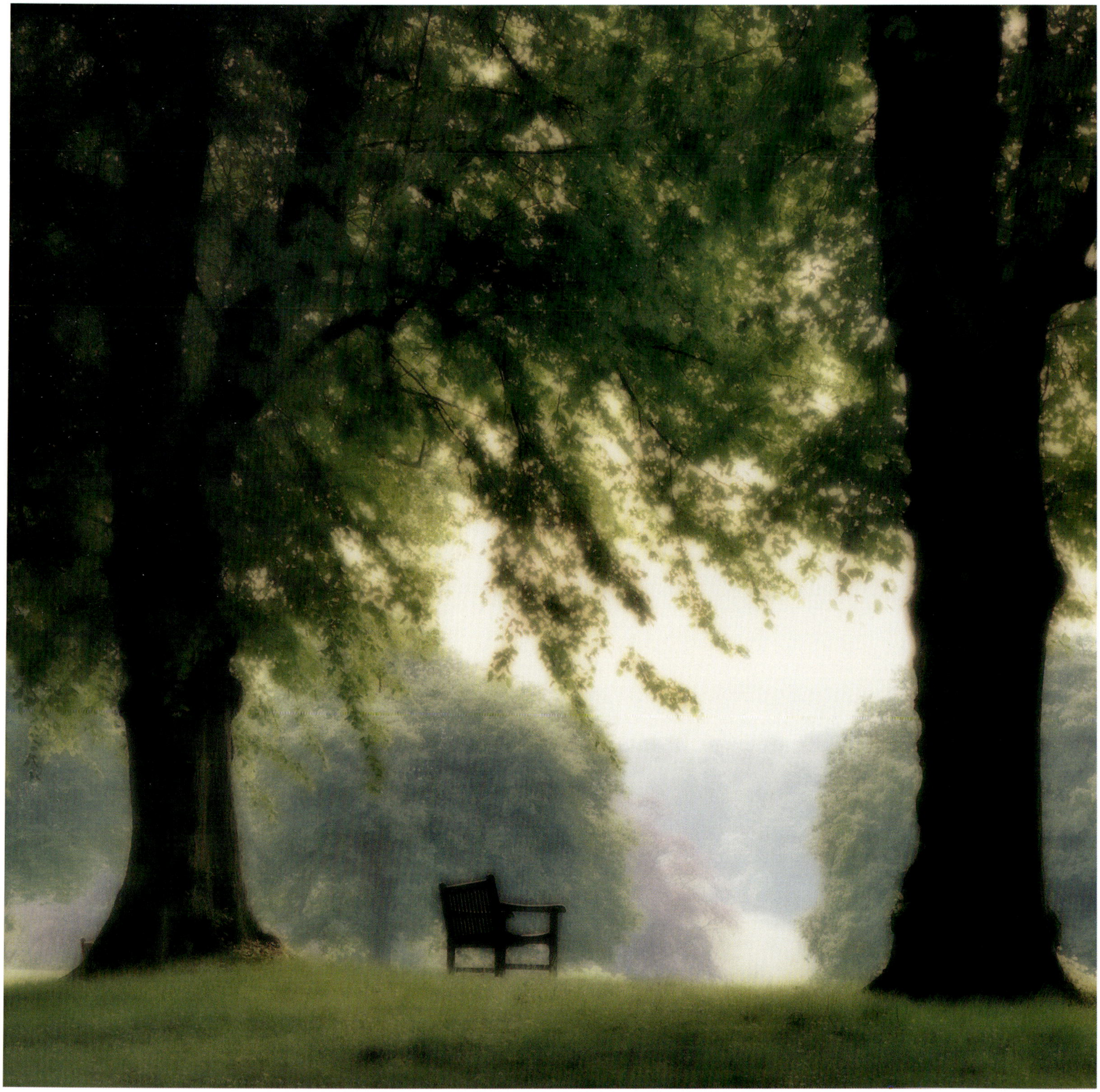

ESSAYS IN ORIENTATION

by Verlyn Klinkenborg

Does it make sense to say "the longing of a path?" To talk about the desire a horizon creates? I think so, and the photographs of Lynn Geesaman prove it. She possesses the discipline that I, as a viewer, always lack: she photographs the depth of a world whose deepness I want to walk into. In the distance, beneath the shade of a German forest, there is a muted green arch of light and a band of sun on the pine thatch, the sign of a natural clearing. In the flat of a Belgian landscape, edged by a canal and overshadowed by trees, a small herd of cows stands at the bend in a track that follows the canal into the mist. The viewer's eye accepts the evidence and the invitation. But the camera doesn't. It stays put. It holds off the horizon, quickening the desire the horizon arouses. It lengthens the path, increasing its longing. Every vertical thrust in these photographs, every colonnade of trees, insists on the way the world recedes from us.

Over the years, I've come to think of Lynn Geesaman's photographs as essays in orientation. This is what I mean. If you've ever been lost in the woods, you know that the problem isn't just losing your way. It's that all ways suddenly look equal. The woods surround you with sameness. Suddenly the only directions that mean anything are the self-referential ones—left and right, front and behind. Oh, there are differences wherever you look, a little more ledge over that way, a tangle of bramble here, some saplings growing in the opening where a tree fell a few years ago. But those differences don't seem to point the way out. You find yourself in a landscape

without strong visual orientation. In other words, not in a landscape at all.

And if you've ever found your way out of the woods after being lost, you know the power of recognition, of realizing where you are. The earth realigns itself. It may be a natural clue that places you, a familiar pool of water or an outcropping of rock. But the clue may also be something artificial in your surroundings, the remains of a stone wall, an orderly massing of shadows in the distance, an unexpected clearing. The dense cross-hatching of limbs begins to thin in front of you, the light changes, and you find yourself looking across a pond through waterside branches at a spreading tree standing alone on the far bank, its reflection filling the middle of the pond. You find yourself looking into the photograph on page 80. You may not know exactly where you are, but you know you're found.

Most of us approach the world of Lynn Geesaman's photographs from a different direction, not from the sameness of the woods but from the sameness of civilization. The intensely ordered landscapes in most of these photographs are nonetheless natural enough to stand for nature itself, for a world utterly beyond the hot asphalt of our daily lives. But the boundlessness of nature, the sense of entanglement in a non-human wilderness, lies well beyond the horizon of most of these landscapes. These images are profoundly imprinted with a sense of path. The nature in these photographs—though you can call it the humanity, too—always directs us. If there's benevolence here, and I think there is, it comes not only from the unmiti-

gated beauty of what Geesaman has to show us but also from the fact that the viewer looks into a world that is intrinsically oriented. The sense of direction is strong, even primary. Each photograph is a study of situation, of being sited. Each photograph is a metaphor for being found in the world.

But the more I look at Geesaman's work, the more I'm struck by the fact that the camera always looks forward. That is obviously a truism. Most cameras can only look forward. Yet no one, to my knowledge, has really been able to describe the way a photograph, looking forward, also captures the photographer who stands behind the camera. Everyone understands the thematic and stylistic coherence that marks a distinctive body of work, the way that what the camera finds identifies the photographer. You can tell a Geesaman photograph at a glance, for instance. But what if we tried to imagine the photographer behind the tripod, tried to think of each of these images as a reverse snapshot of the photographer at work, a forward-positive in which the negative would look backward?

I know it's a question worth asking because in my conversations with Geesaman, I've heard her use the word "desperate," which is a word you'd never conjure for yourself by looking at these photographs. She means, to begin with, a photographer's desperation, a certainty that the exact thing she was looking for has swum into her viewfinder and has to be caught before it vanishes. She suffers every photographer's anxiety about the coming and going of light, about mobile obstructions, like humans, that wander into the line of sight

and immobile ones, like signs identifying the plants in formal gardens. She knows, as every artist does, that assurance can vanish in a heartbeat and return a heartbeat too late.

But to utter another truism, these photographs place the photographer in the settings where they were shot. The photographs take the immediacy of the moment and transform it into something lasting. But the immediacy—what it was like to be there—remains in the photographer's memory, though it's something we've taught ourselves to believe is irrelevant to any formal consideration of the work at hand. I've been surprised, in talking with Geesaman, to realize that when she's working in the field she often feels dislocated. Instead of being enveloped by the world she photographs, she holds it literally at arm's length, in the waist-level viewfinder of her camera, which she uses as a visual compass, guiding her as she walks. When she talks about working in these gardens and formal landscapes, her voice often contains an intimation of trespass, as if someone had been waiting to evict her the moment she planted her tripod. (Sometimes someone has.) The weather and the season and, in some cases, the very foreignness of the setting bear down on her. No amount of research will waylay a feeling of unfamiliarity, and no degree of familiarity will dissipate the sense of displacement that making a photograph causes.

Dislocation, displacement, desperation: these are strange words to describe the artistic backdrop to these images because they create, above all, a feeling of location and placement, an order that is as

emotional as it is visual. I don't want to suggest a simple inversion here, as though the tranquility of these photographs necessarily mirrored Geesaman's sense of displacement. But in the artist's search for these images I believe there is also a search for orientation. To be just short of the perfection you're seeking, as an artist, is a place of enormous tension. Something in the scene stops Geesaman in her tracks. Something stills the camera and releases the shutter.

To me that momentary tension is the clue to these photographs. It's always tempting to look at the formality they depict—the avenues of trees, the symmetry of the designed landscape—as a kind of repose, as if order were merely rest or inertia. But what Geesaman sees is that order of this kind is also tension. In the most rigidly formal settings, in Parc de Sceaux or Parc de Canon, the trees bristle with energy. They stand their ground. They quiver with height. They keep their proper distance. And when the settings are less formal, when a tree in leaf stands alone in the foreground, it's as though it had wandered cautiously toward the photographer from among the company of its peers and was about to vanish at the sound of the shutter. I exaggerate the animation of the objects in these landscapes but not their dynamism. To photograph this deeply hidden principle of formality is what Geesaman means when she says that her photographs re-order the ordered landscape. I would say it a different way. Her photographs know what order means.

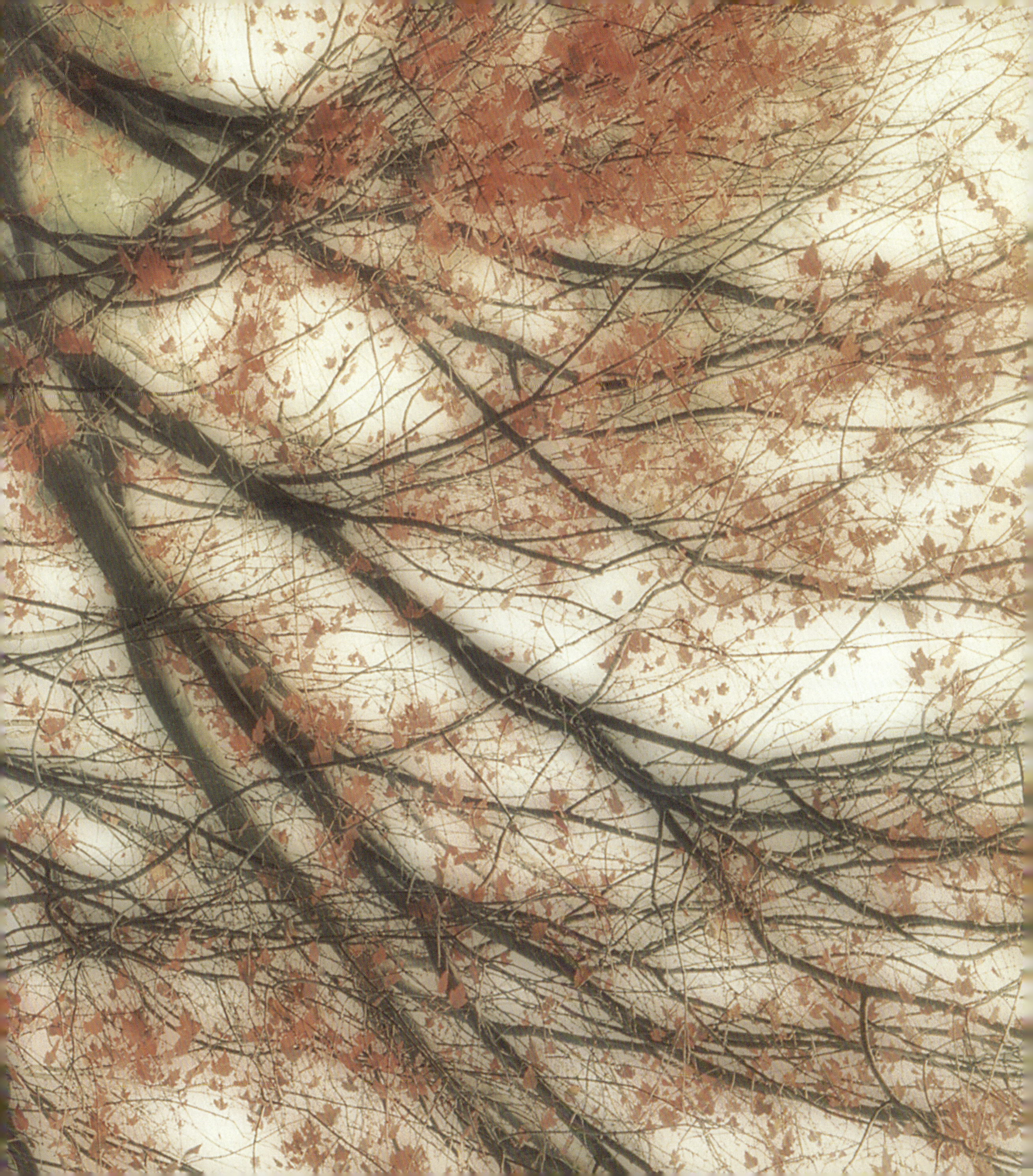

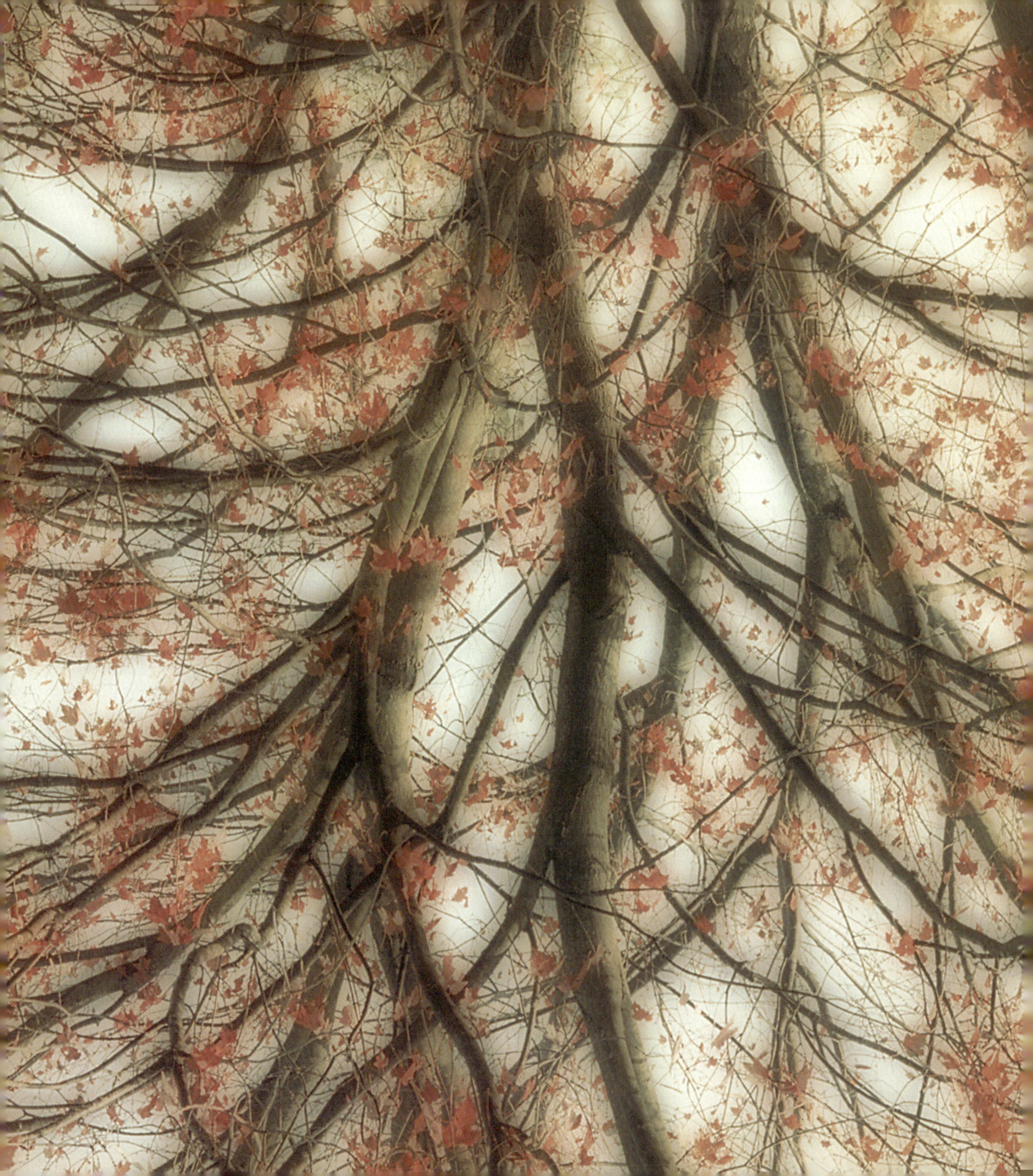

The lone tree fits perfectly into a sliver of gold rape field on this hill in Scotland. The catenary below buoys it up into the evening sky.

Tayside, Scotland, 1994

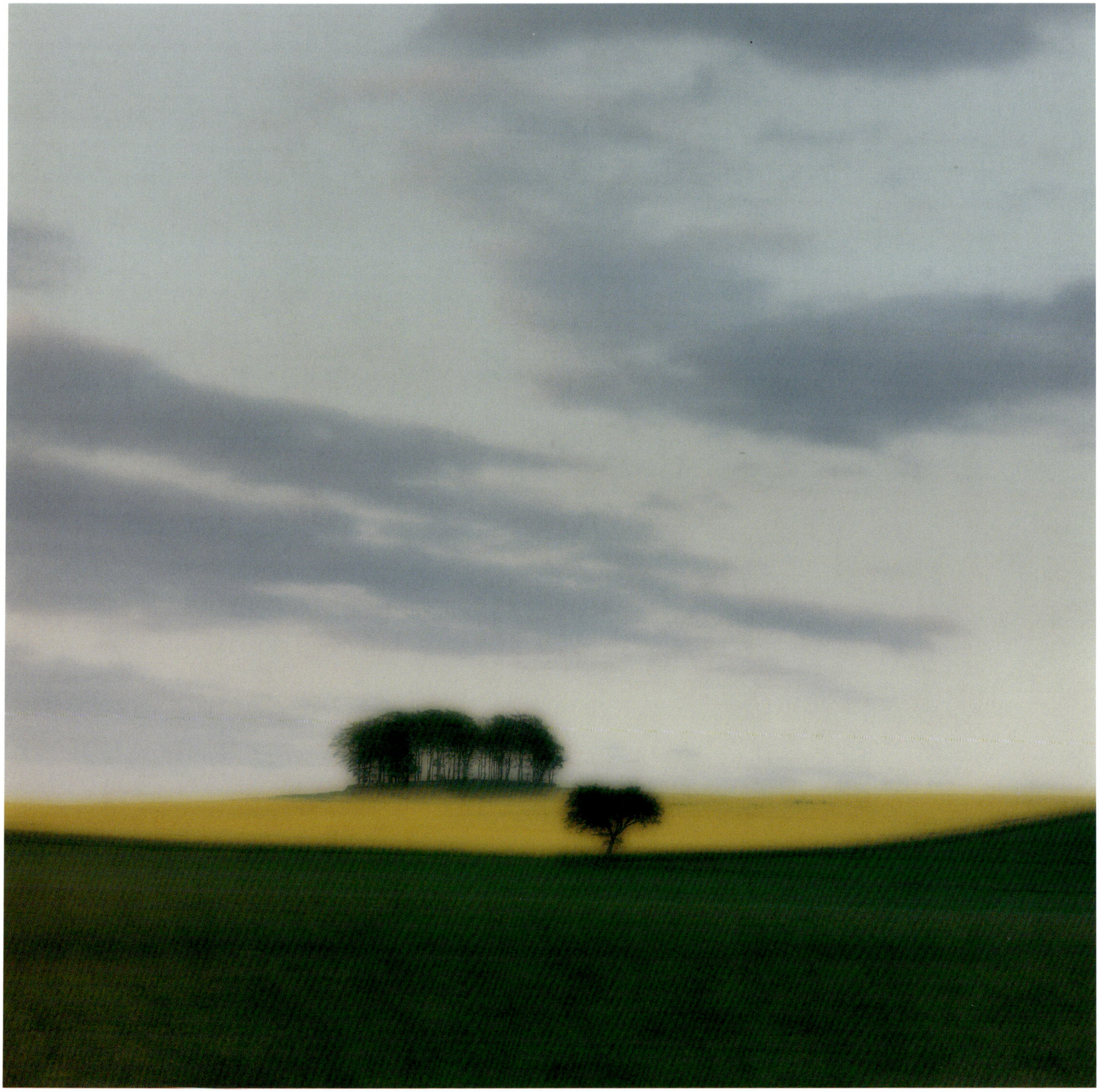

Güstrow, Germany, 1993

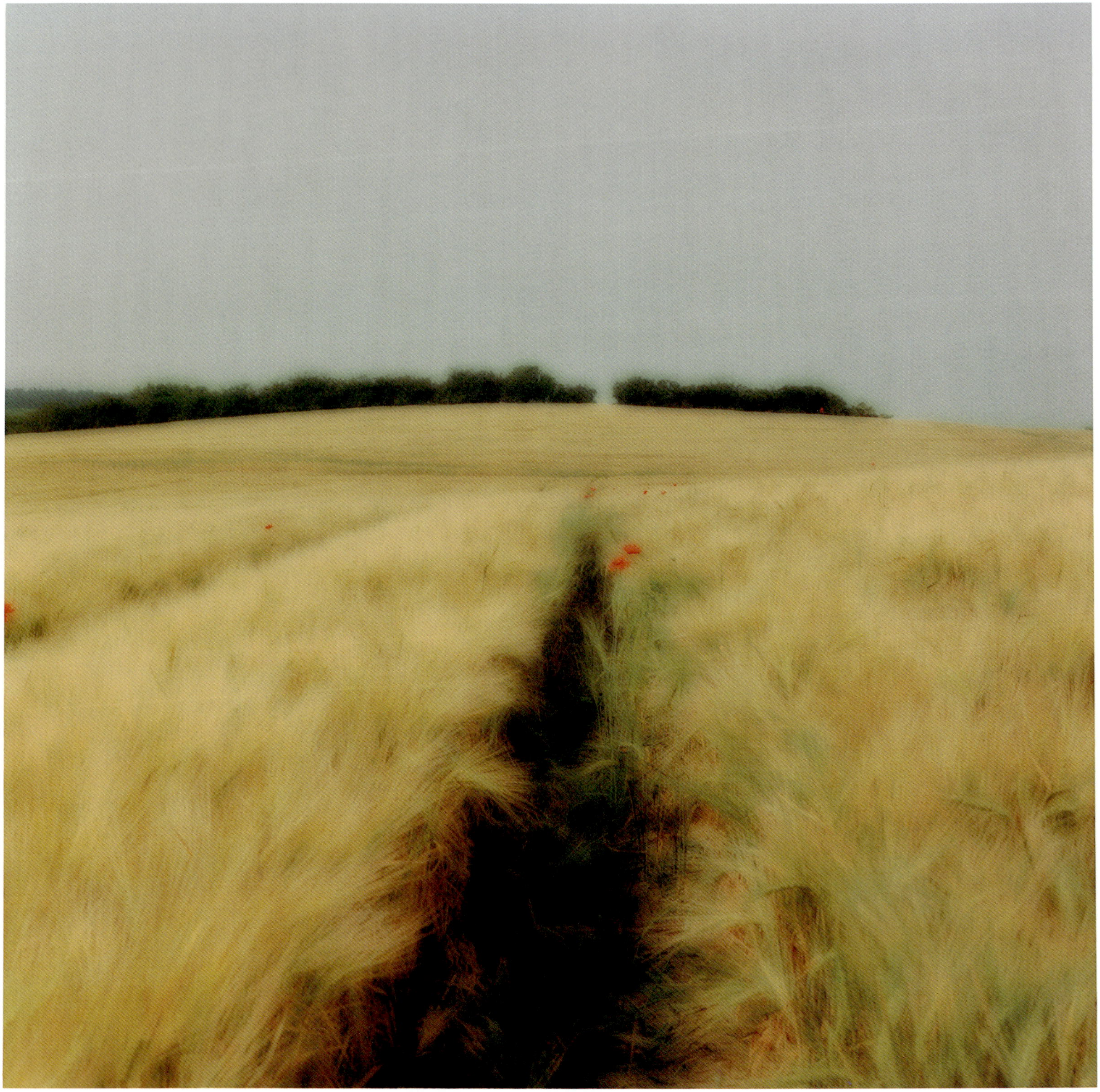

Crathes Castle Garden, near Aberdeen, Scotland, 1994

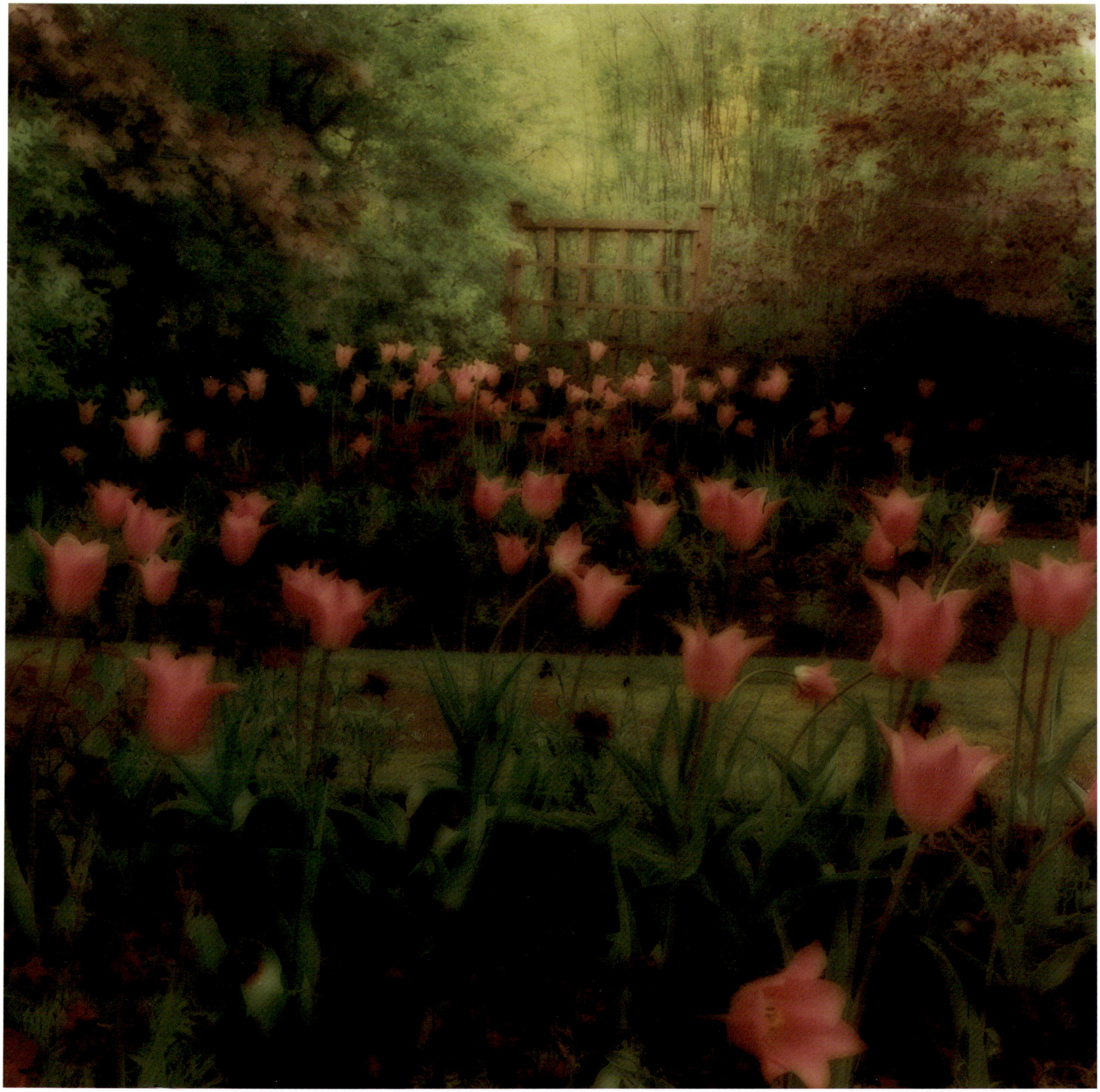

Crarae Glen Garden, Argyll, Scotland, 1994

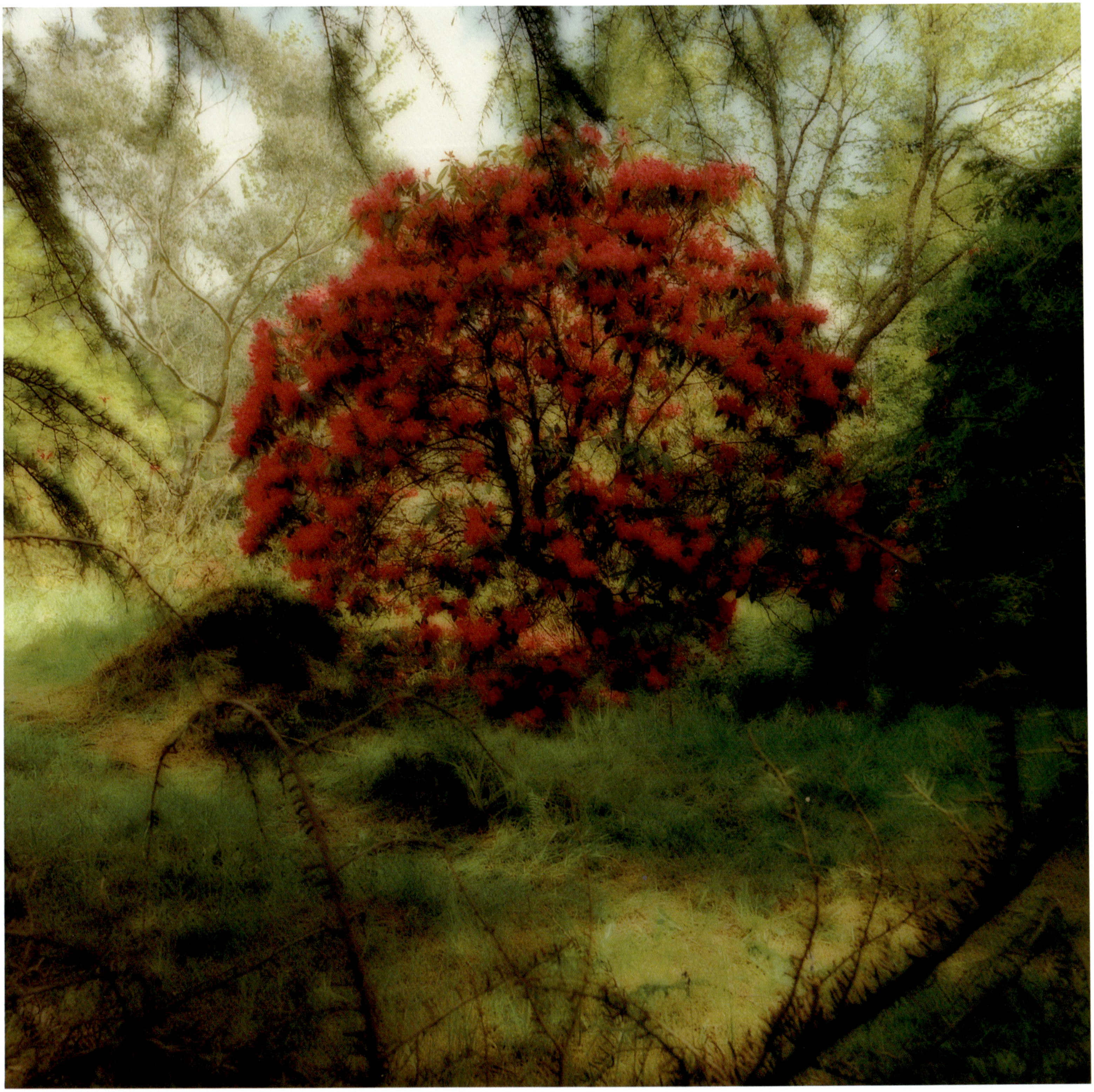

Red tulips march in military order before a backdrop of trees with the shapes of bonsai. Neither would do well without the other.

Parc de Bagatelle, Paris, France, 1995

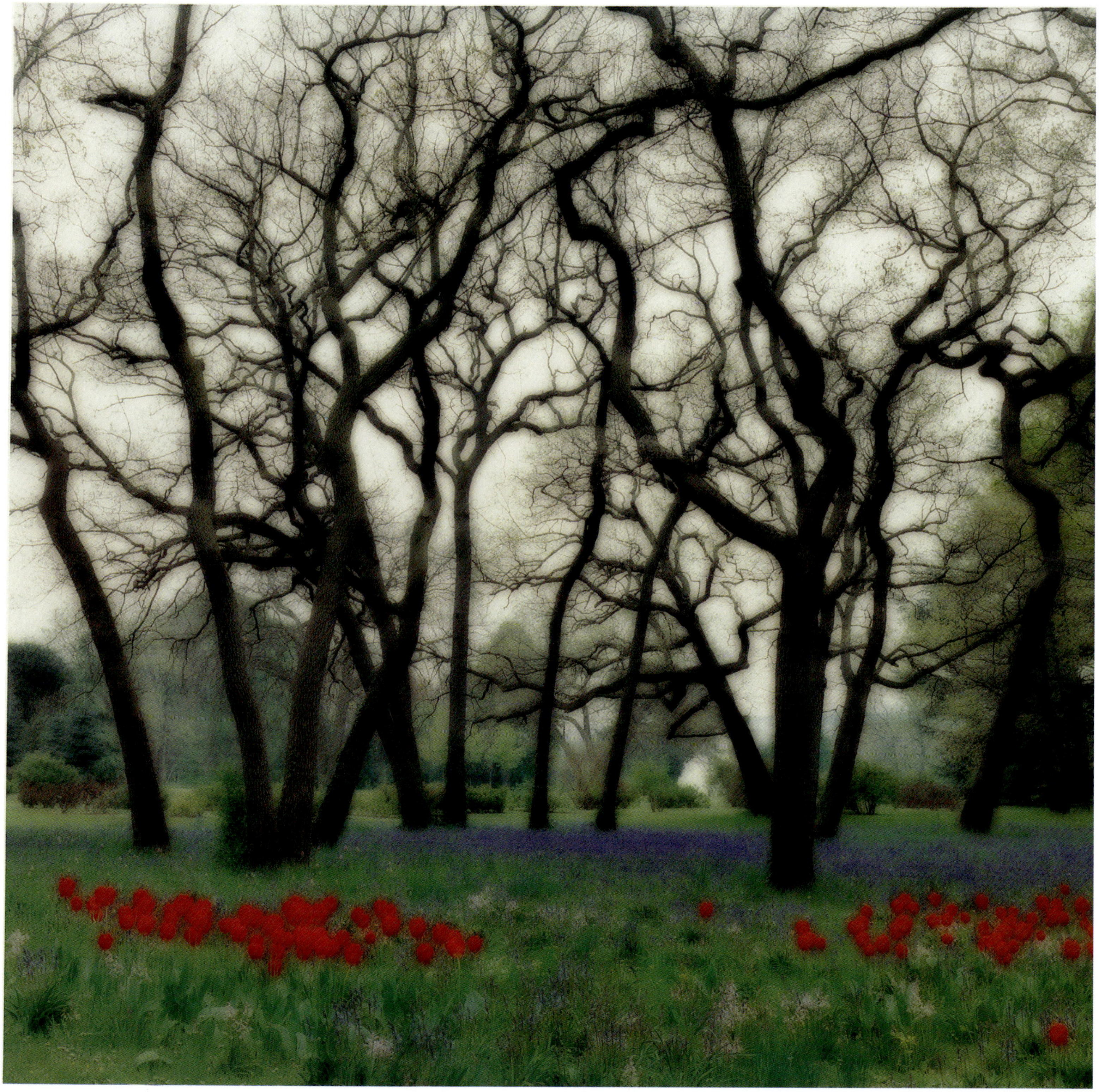

Parc de Canon, near Caen, France, 1995

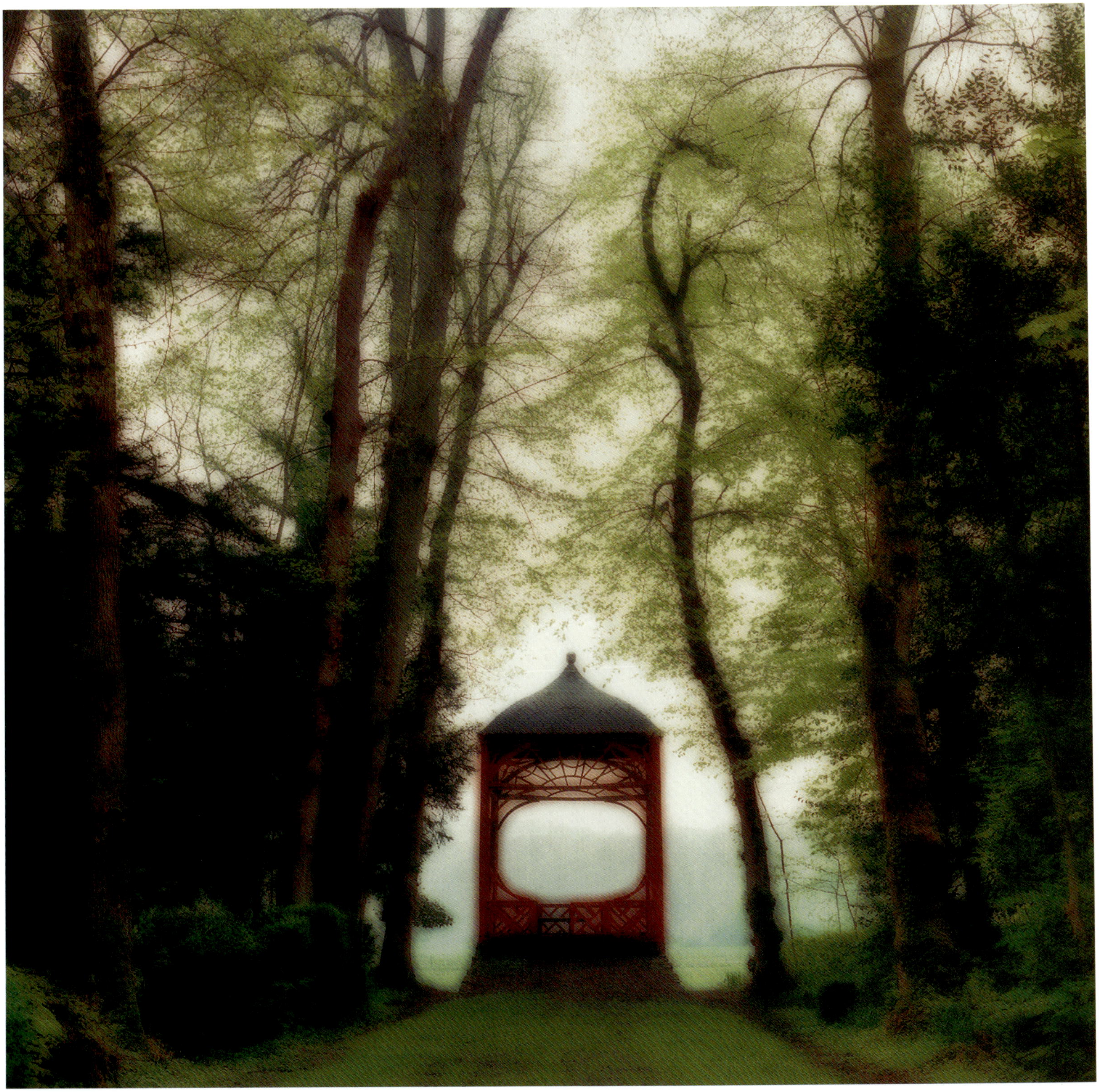

Making this photograph was like standing backstage in a theater.
I looked beyond dark shapes into the pale pastel light
of a classic Normandy garden near Caen.

Parc de Canon, near Caen, France, 1995

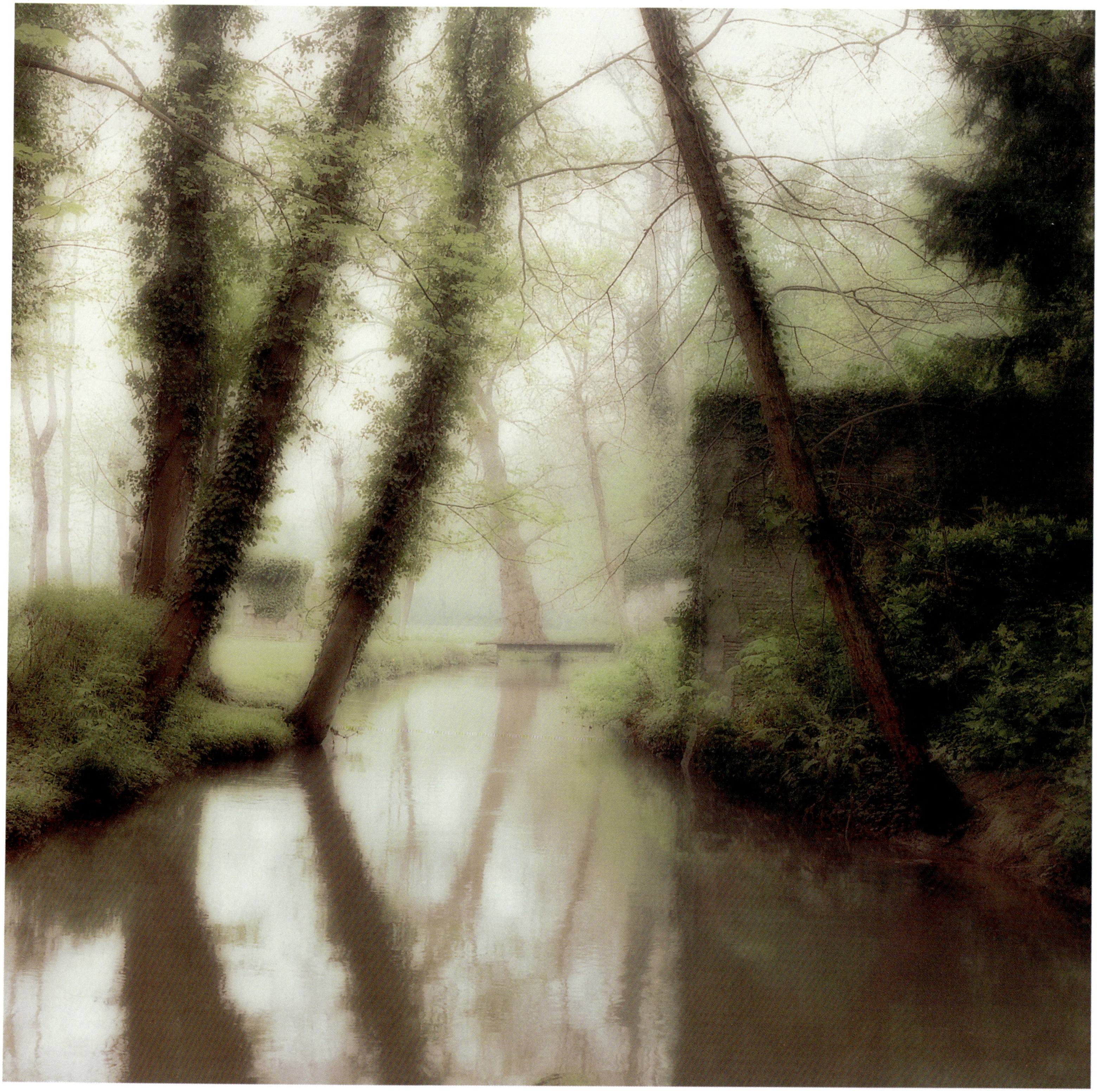

The trees seem pinched together at the top forming a graceful natural framing. I like the lush grassy ground in the foreground, more like lawn than the allée of a formal garden. The horticultural influences here are both French and English.

Parc de Canon, near Caen, France, 1995

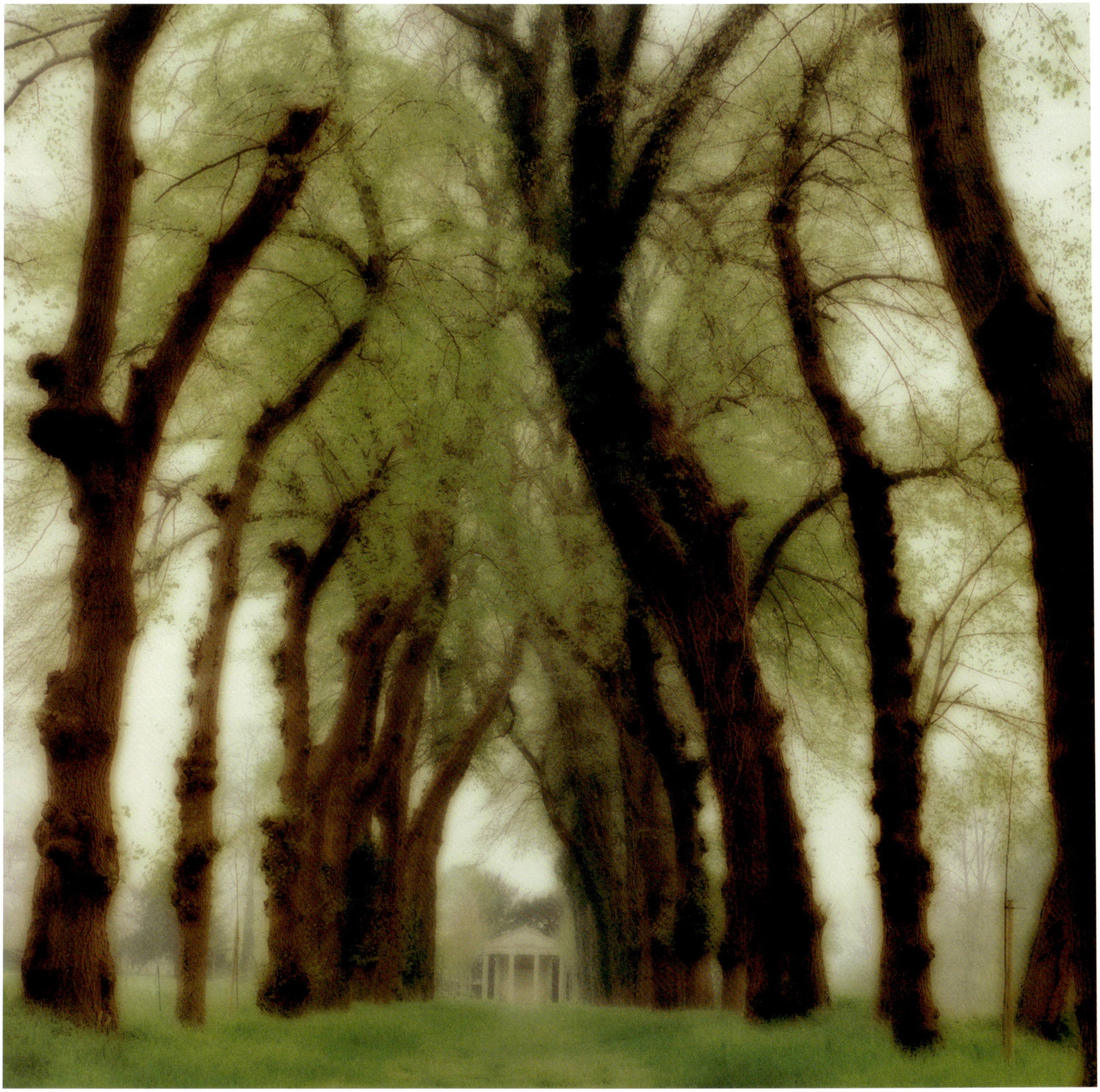

Forêt de Cerisy, Normandy, France, 1995

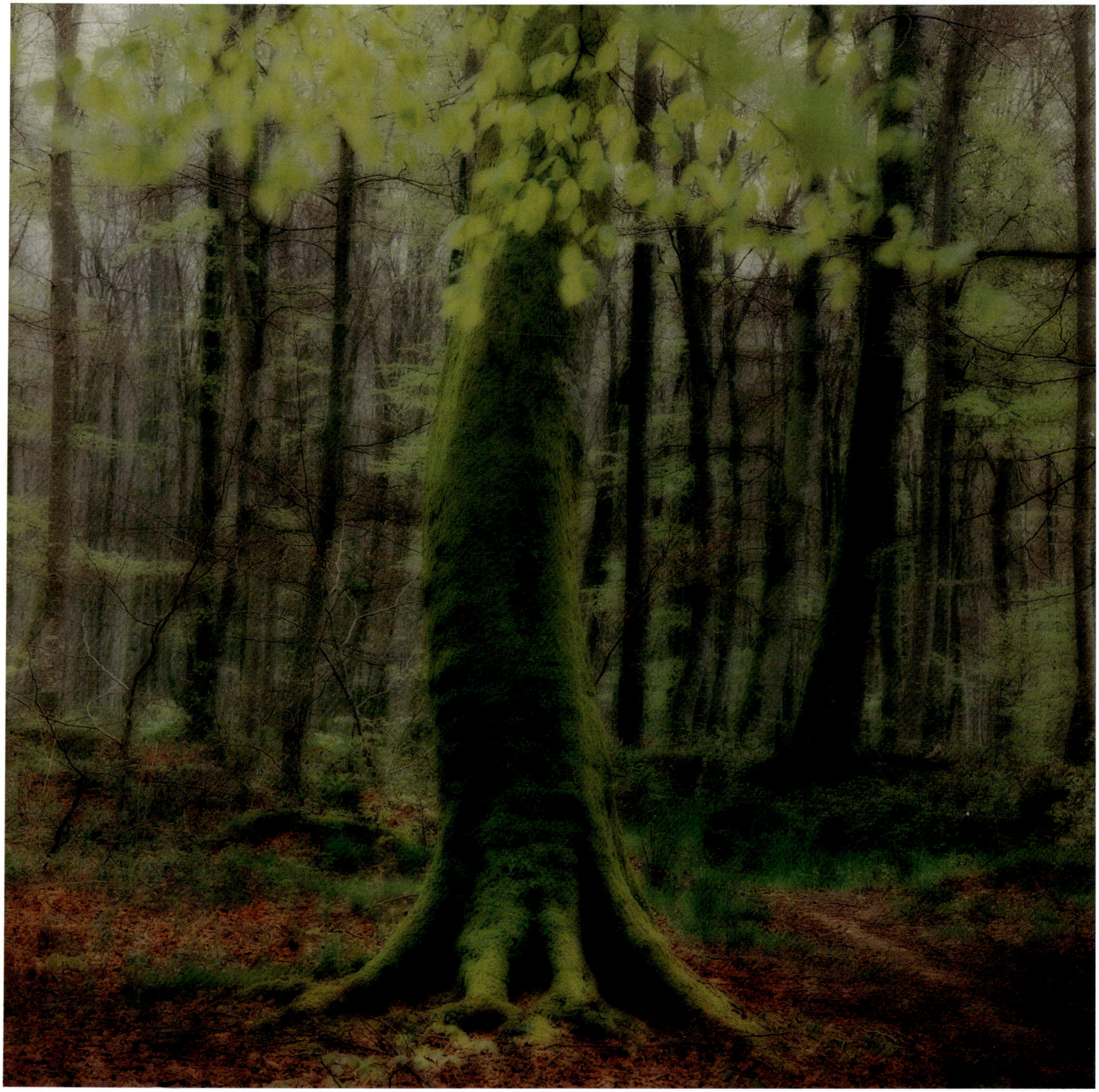

These allées of cut trees are magical in any season. Here I was working with almost solid shapes, but the blazing autumn color comes through, and the geometries are perfectly balanced. I particularly like the turquoise and orange in the lower right area.

Parc de Sceaux, near Paris, France, 1997

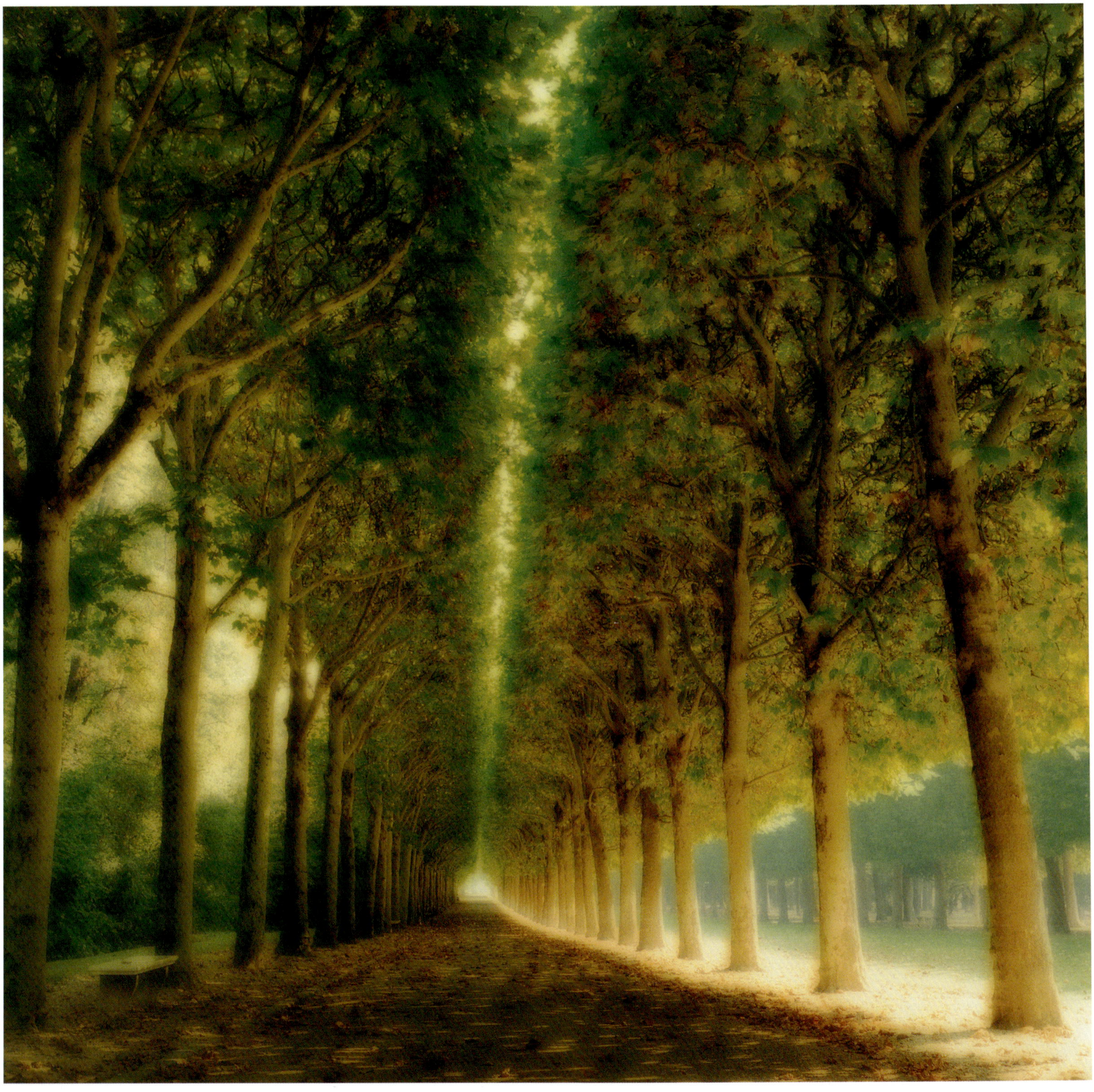

Parc de Sceaux, near Paris, France, 1995

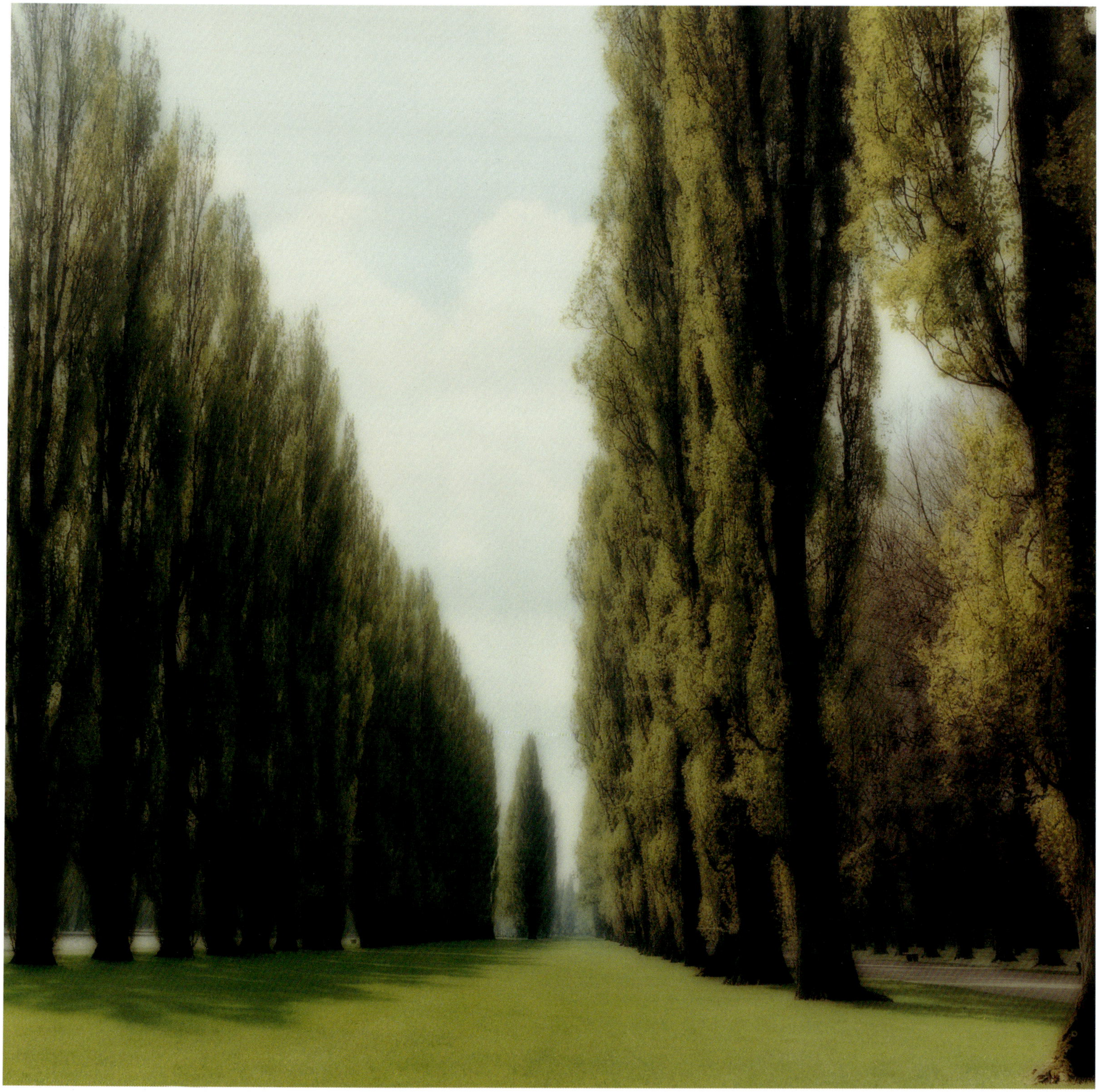

The pure geometry of a seventeenth-century French park: a haze of yellow buds softens the ends of the branches, an effect that enhances an otherwise severe subject. Of the many places I have photographed in Europe, this park, south of Paris, is a longtime favorite.

Parc de Sceaux, near Paris, France, 1995

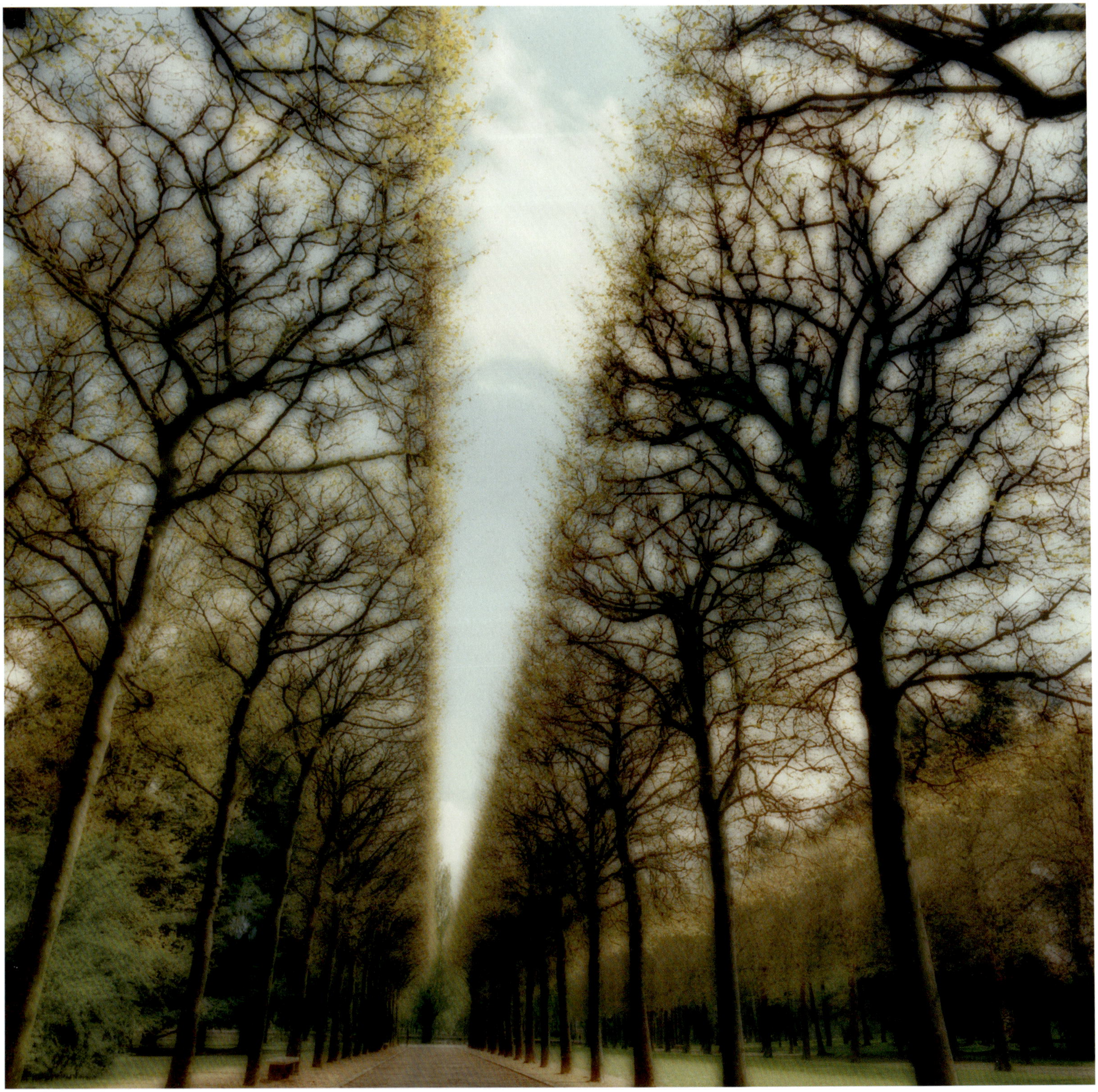

Parc de Sceaux, near Paris, France, 1995

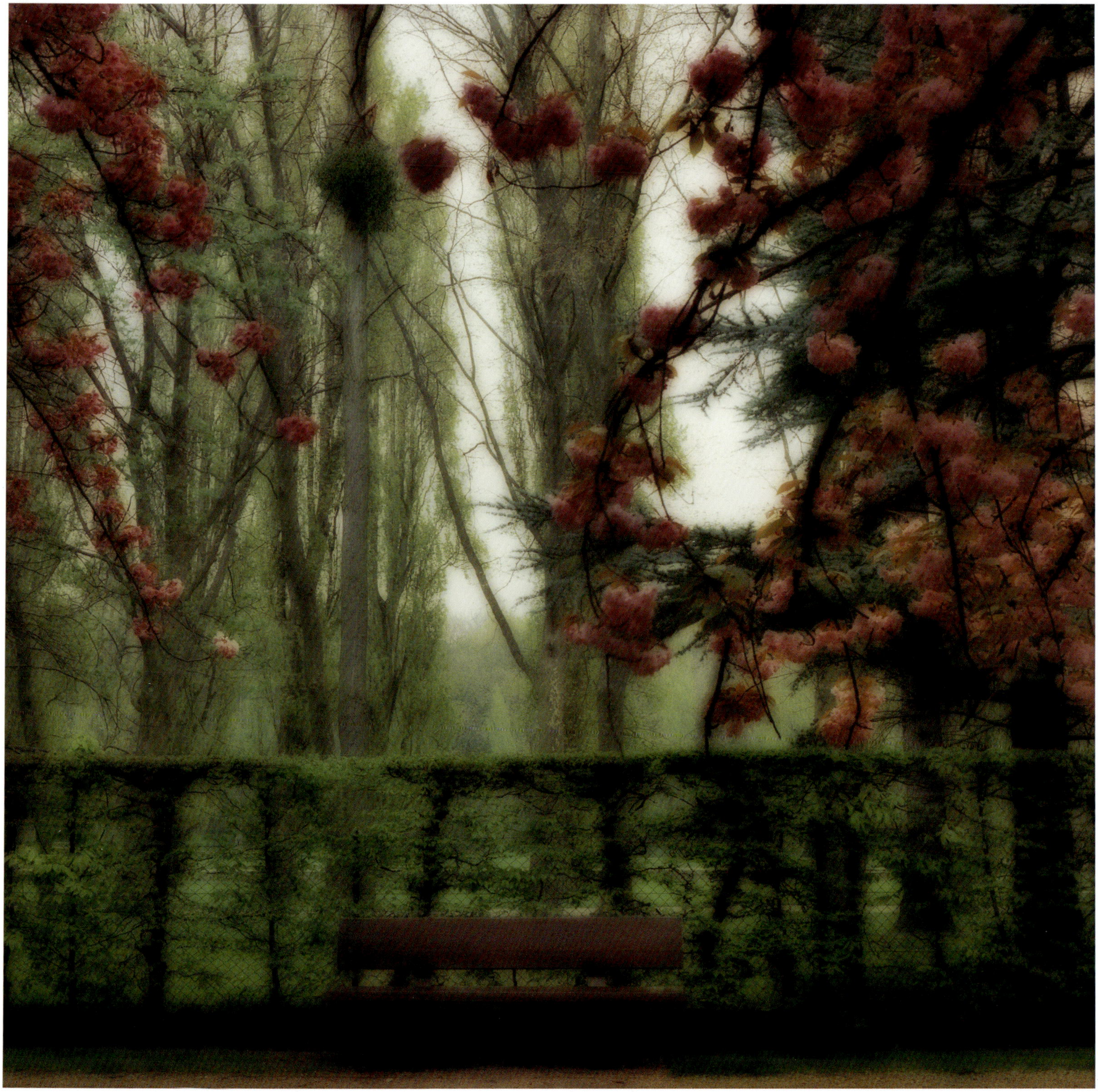

Parc de Bagatelle, Paris, France, 1995

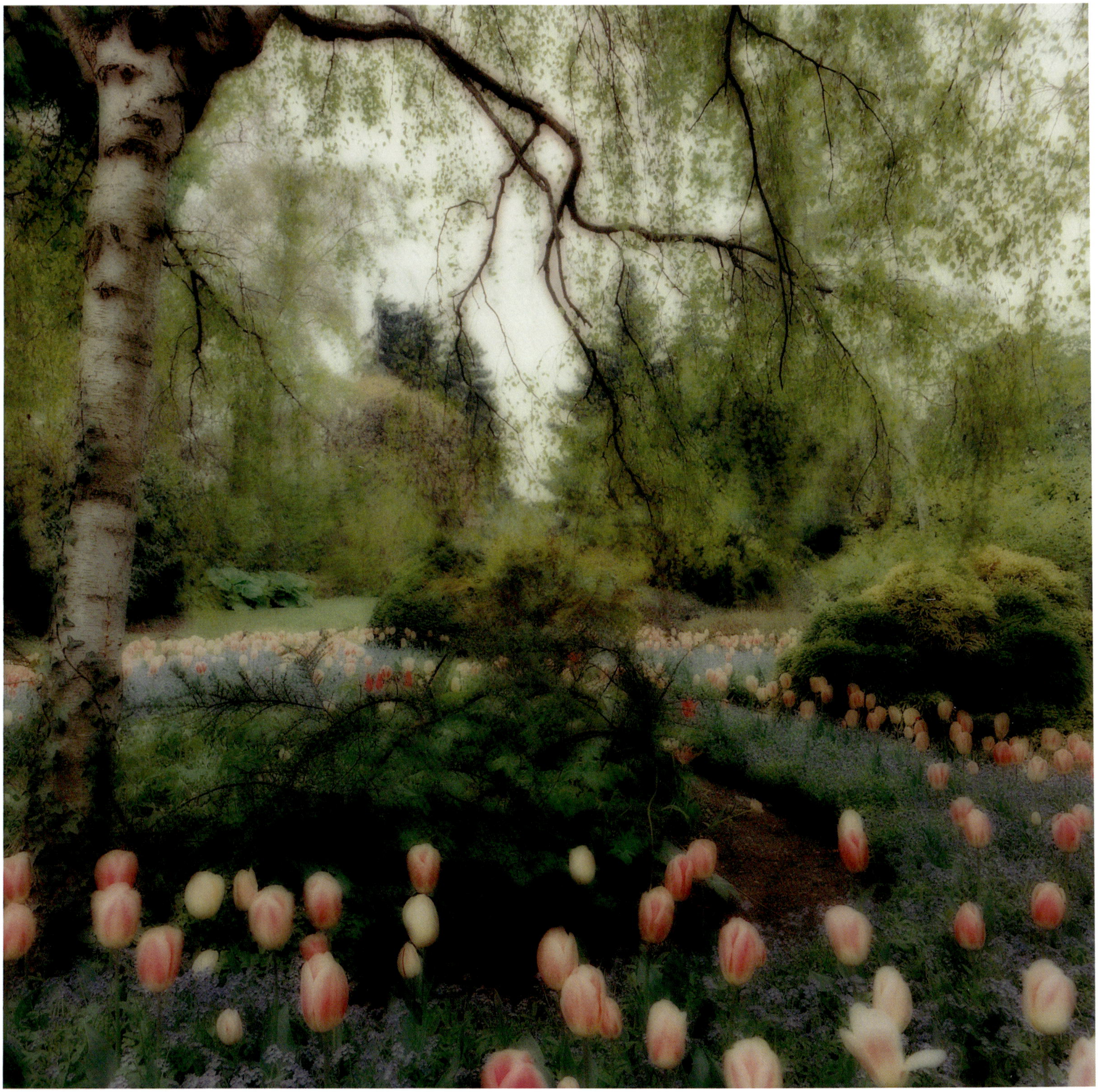

Parc de Bagatelle, Paris, France, 1995

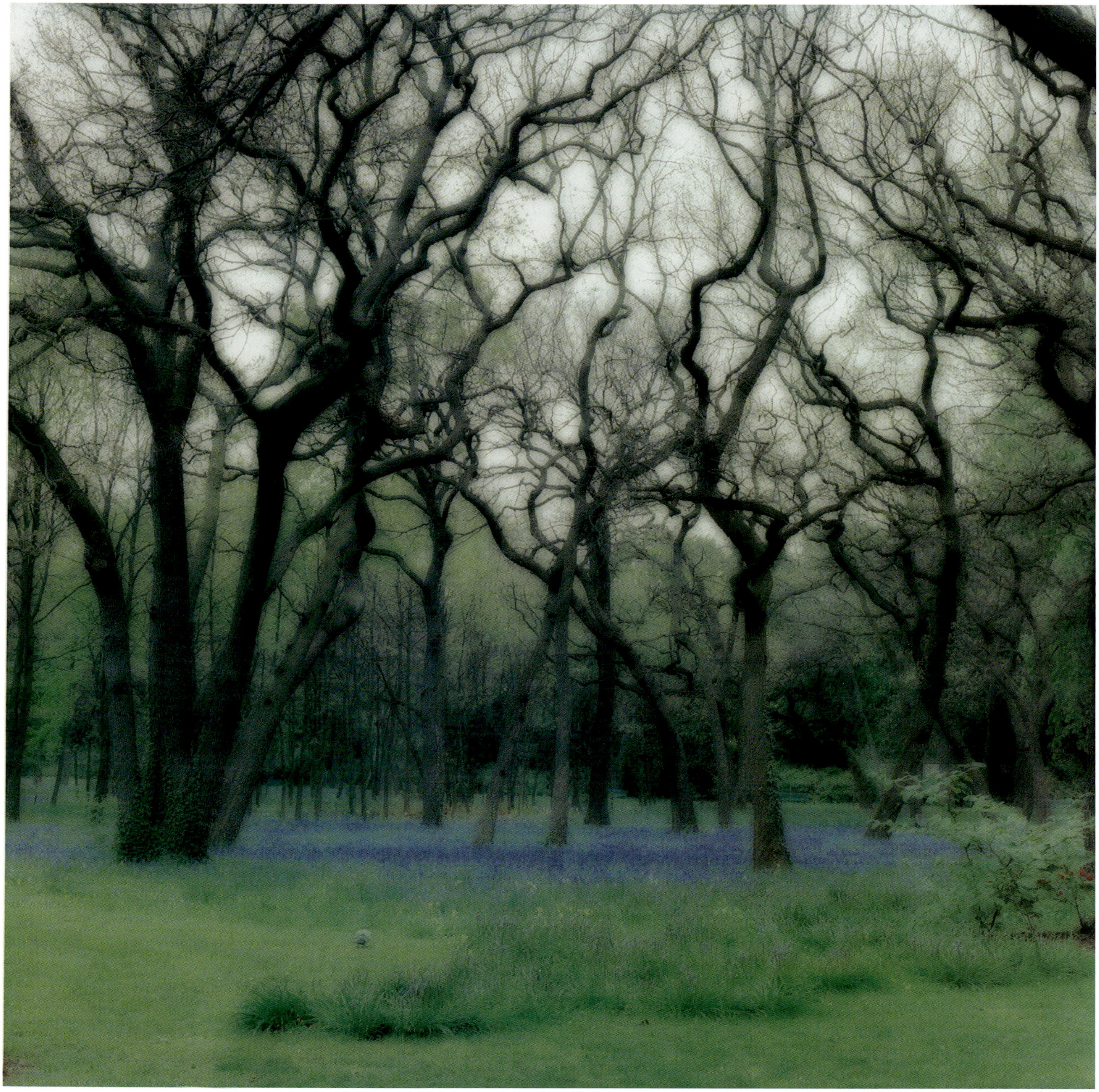

Andalucia, Spain, 2002

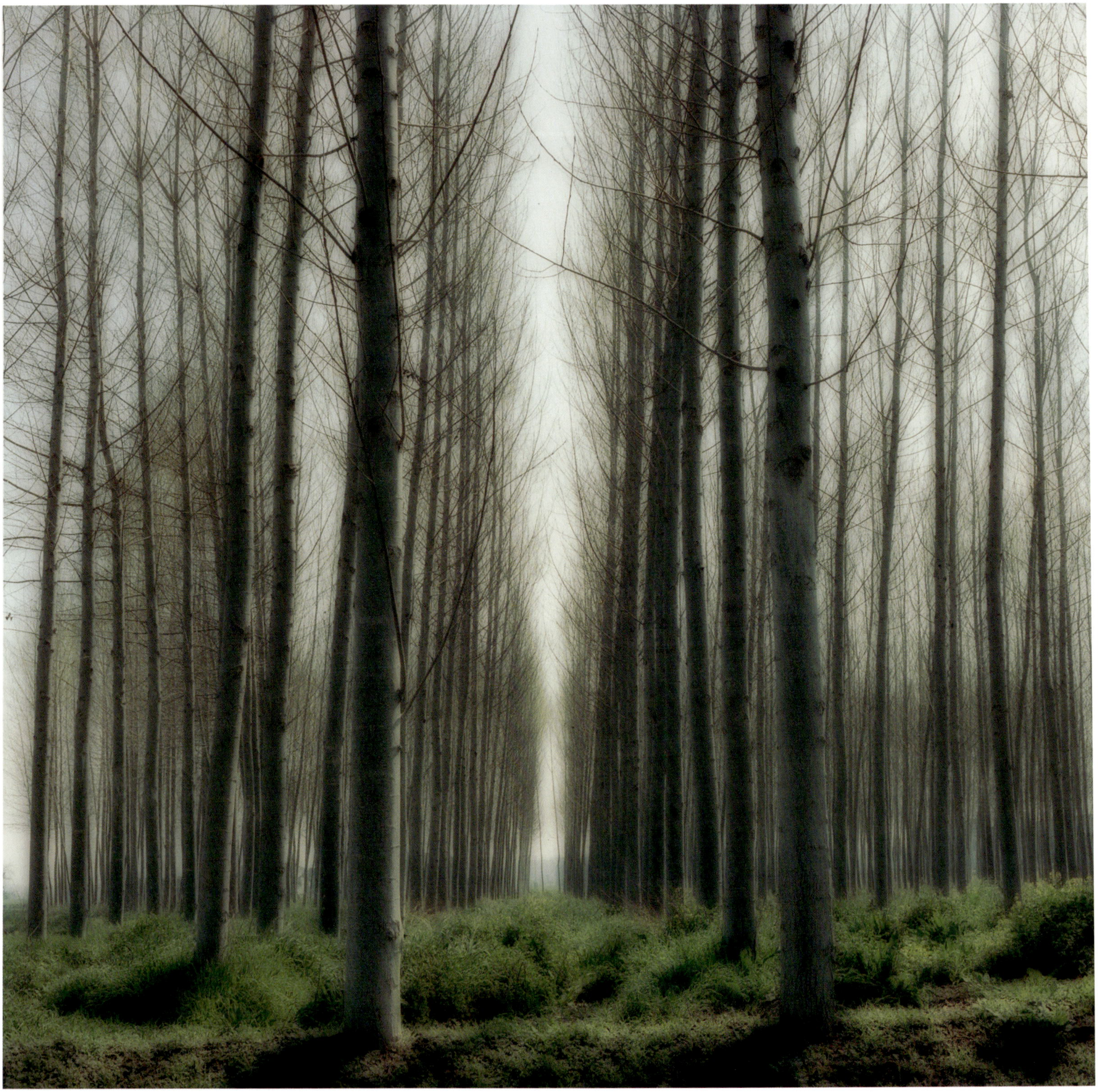

Parc de Jeurre, Morigny-Champigny, France, 1999

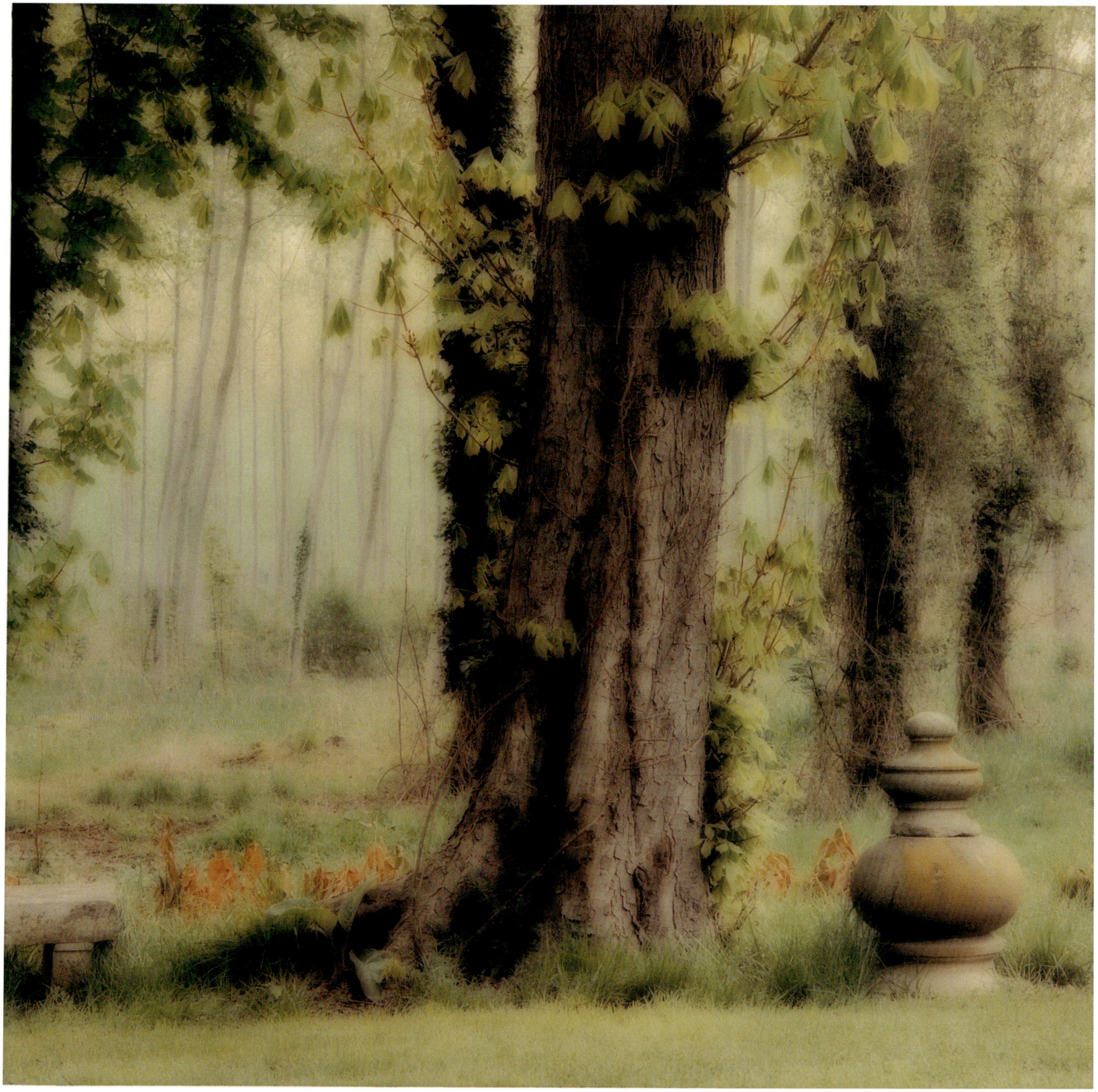

Parc de Jeurre, Morigny-Champigny, France, 1999

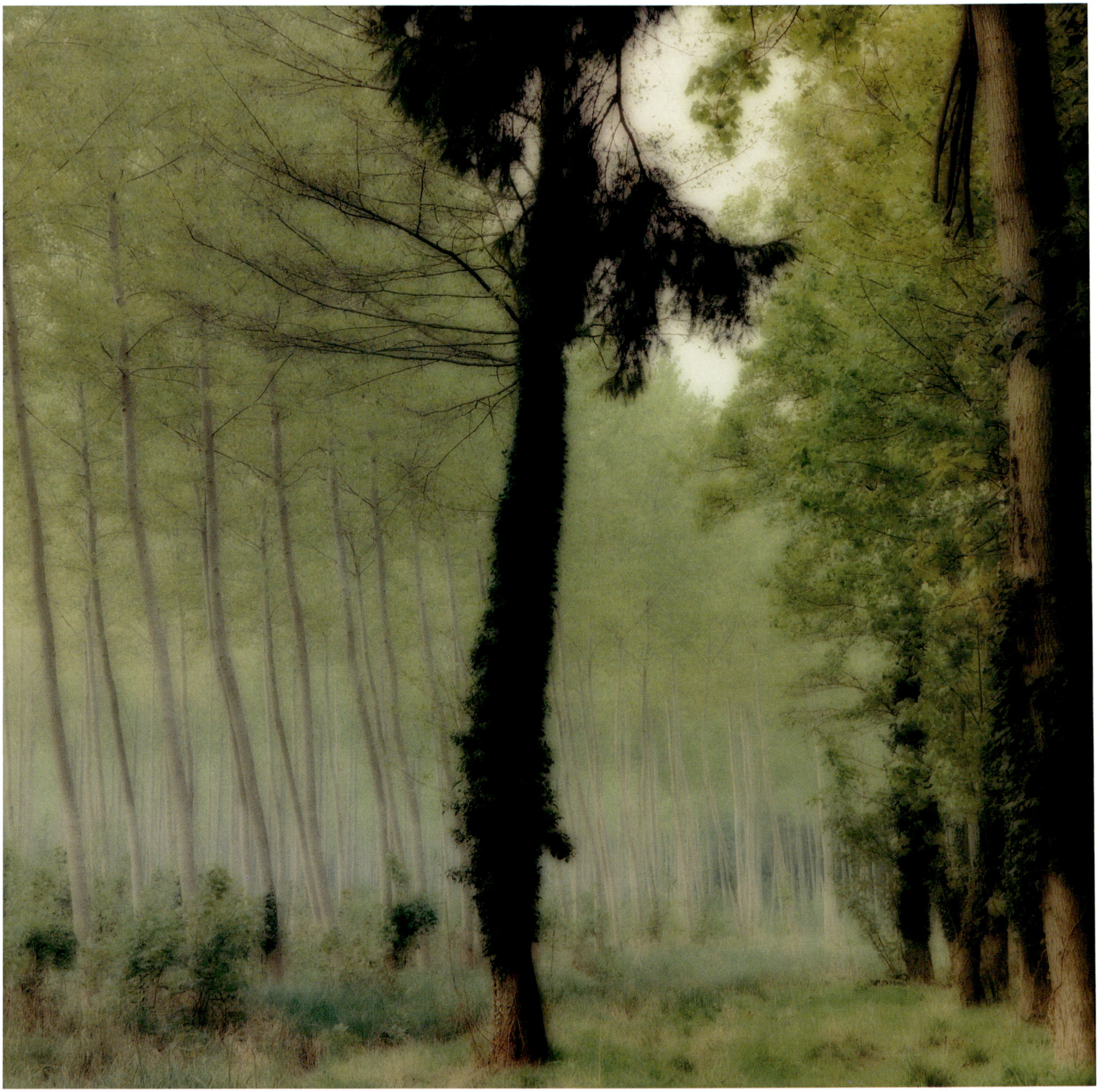

It's a good thing I like the darkroom because it's a huge part of what I do. This is possibly the most sublime tree picture I've ever found. In printing it, I discovered latent blue and pink by subtracting some of the obvious yellow and green. A triumph! I'd like to take all the credit but I could only resurrect what was at the park and was recorded on film that particular day.

Parc de Jeurre, Morigny-Champigny, France, 1999

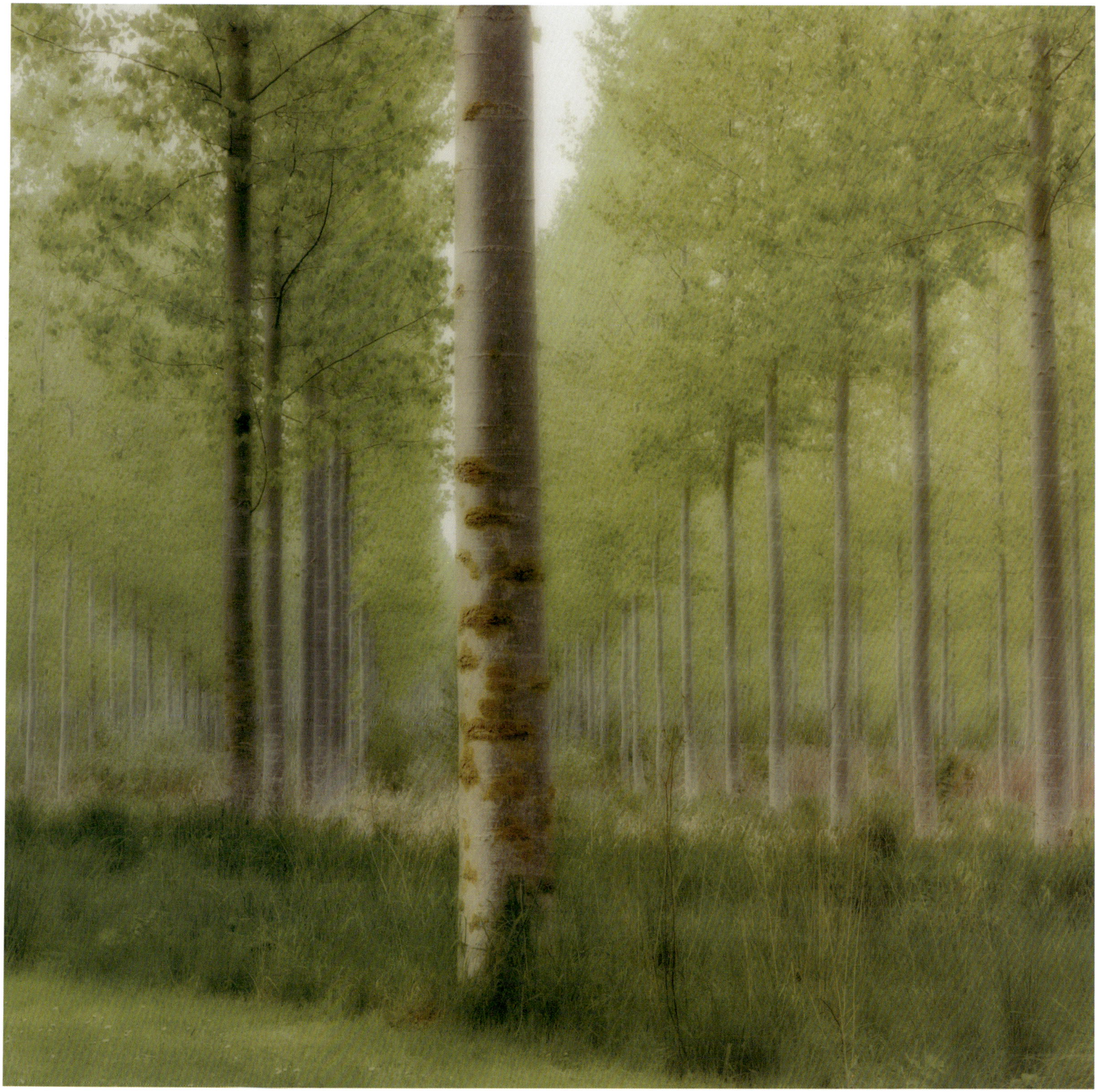

In France, this is not a haphazard arrangement: the tiny dark conical topiary appears to be both a source of light and the origin of lines of force that radiate out. This day I forgot my lens shade, but it proved for the best; the midday flare was magical.

Parc de Bagatelle, Paris, France, 1997

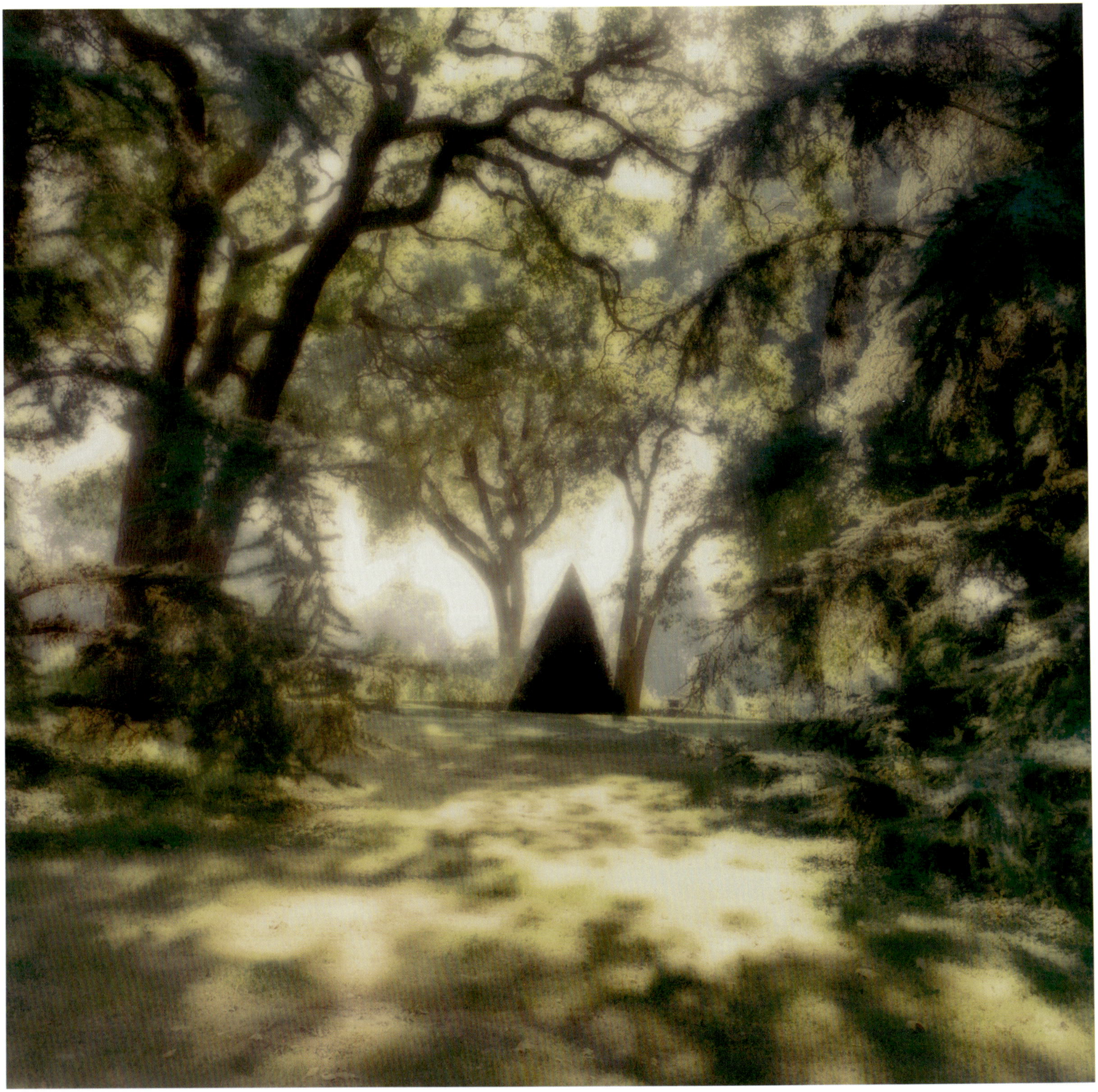

Fog has settled on the canals at the Chateau d'Esclimont. The early morning sun behind the topiaries delineated their shapes and threw long shadows. This property, between Chartres and Versailles, belonged to the Rochefoucauld family.

Parc d'Esclimont, near Versailles, France, 1999

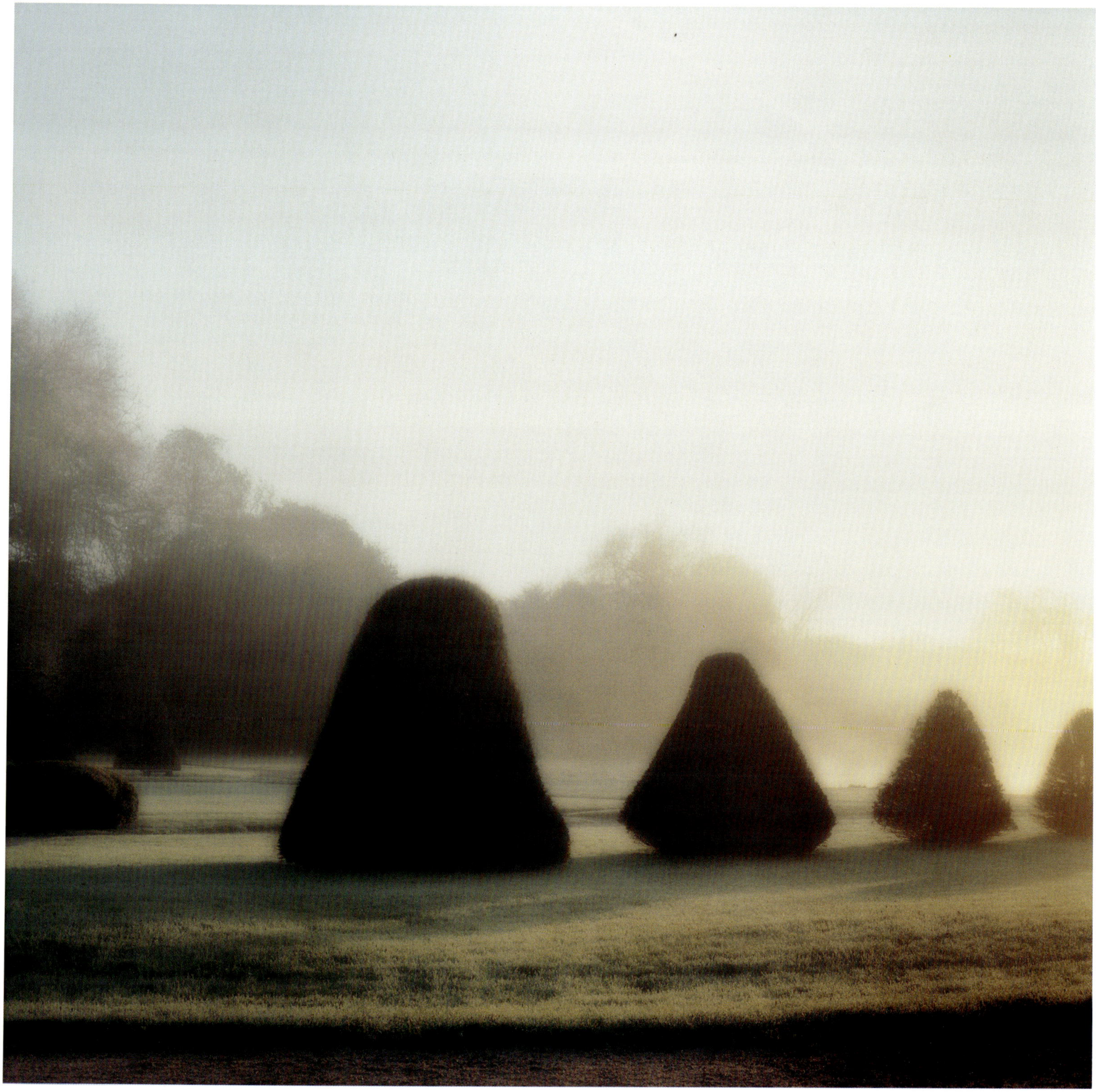

Luxembourg Gardens, Paris, France, 1997

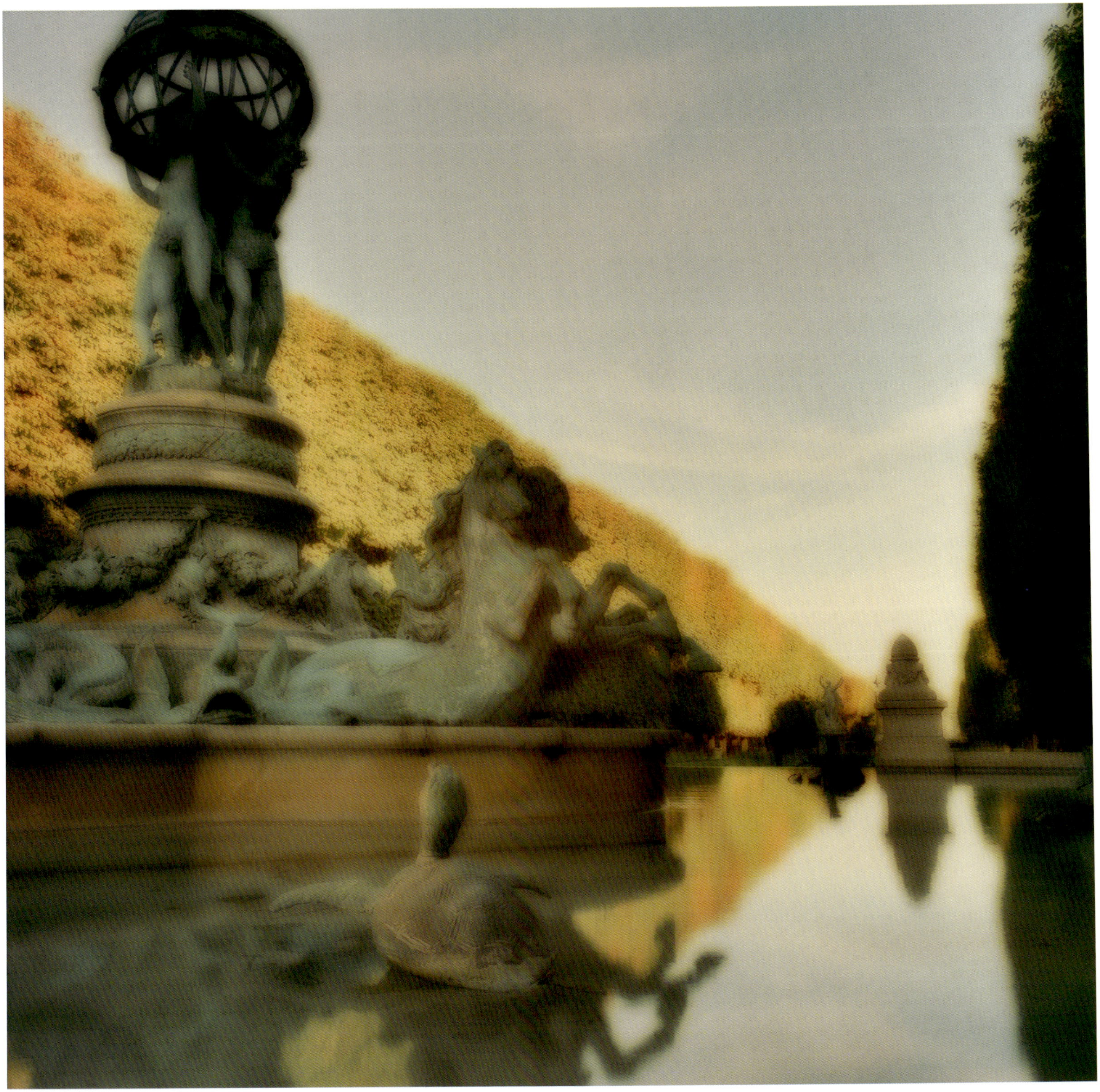

Parc d'Esclimont, near Versailles, France, 1995

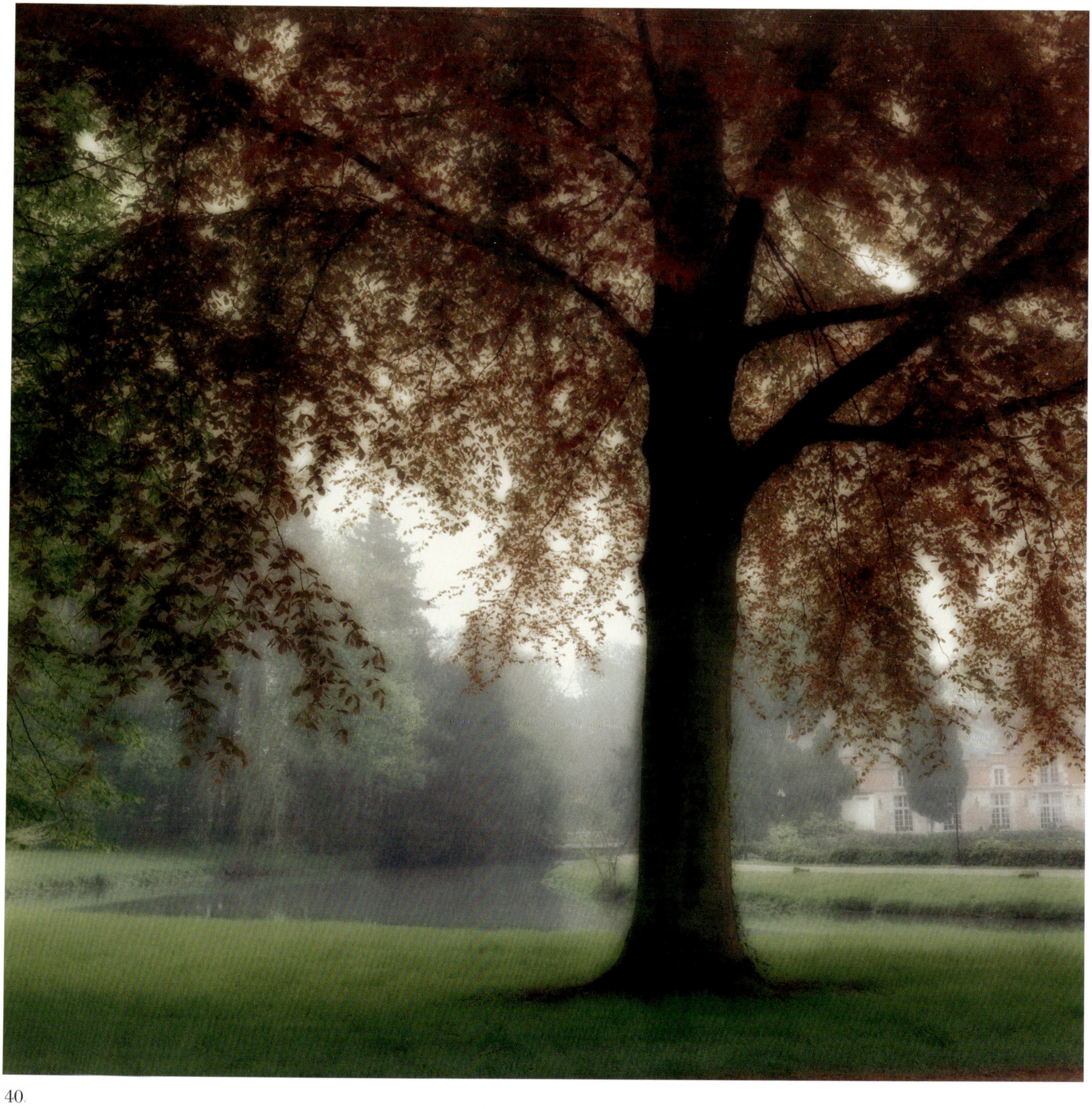

Damme, near Bruges, Belgium, 1995

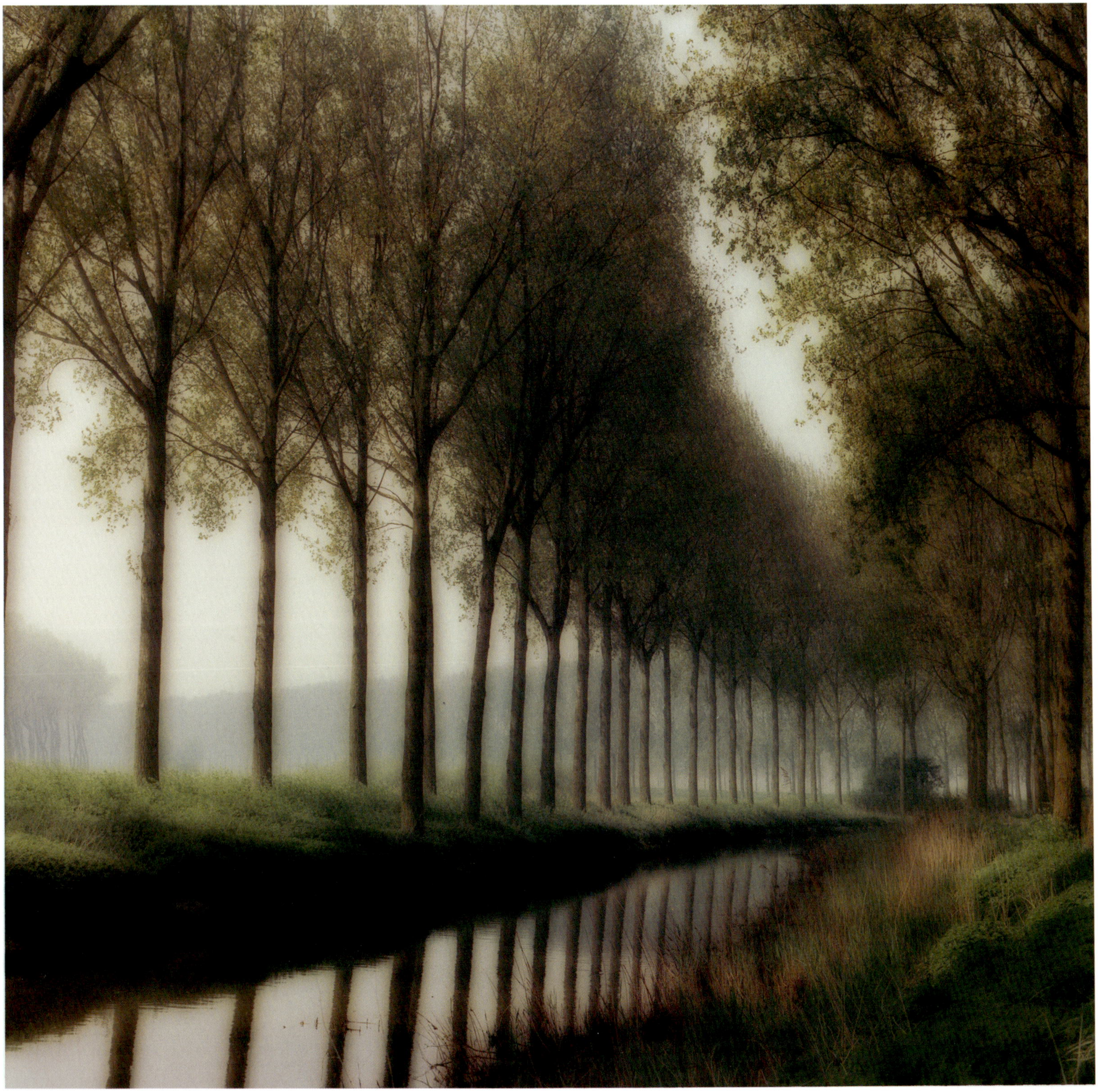

Versatile and unique as a landscape, this canal region north of Bruges contains rows of regularly spaced trees along winding canals. From a distance, you can see that the trees are bent from the wind off the North Sea.

Damme, near Bruges, Belgium, 1995

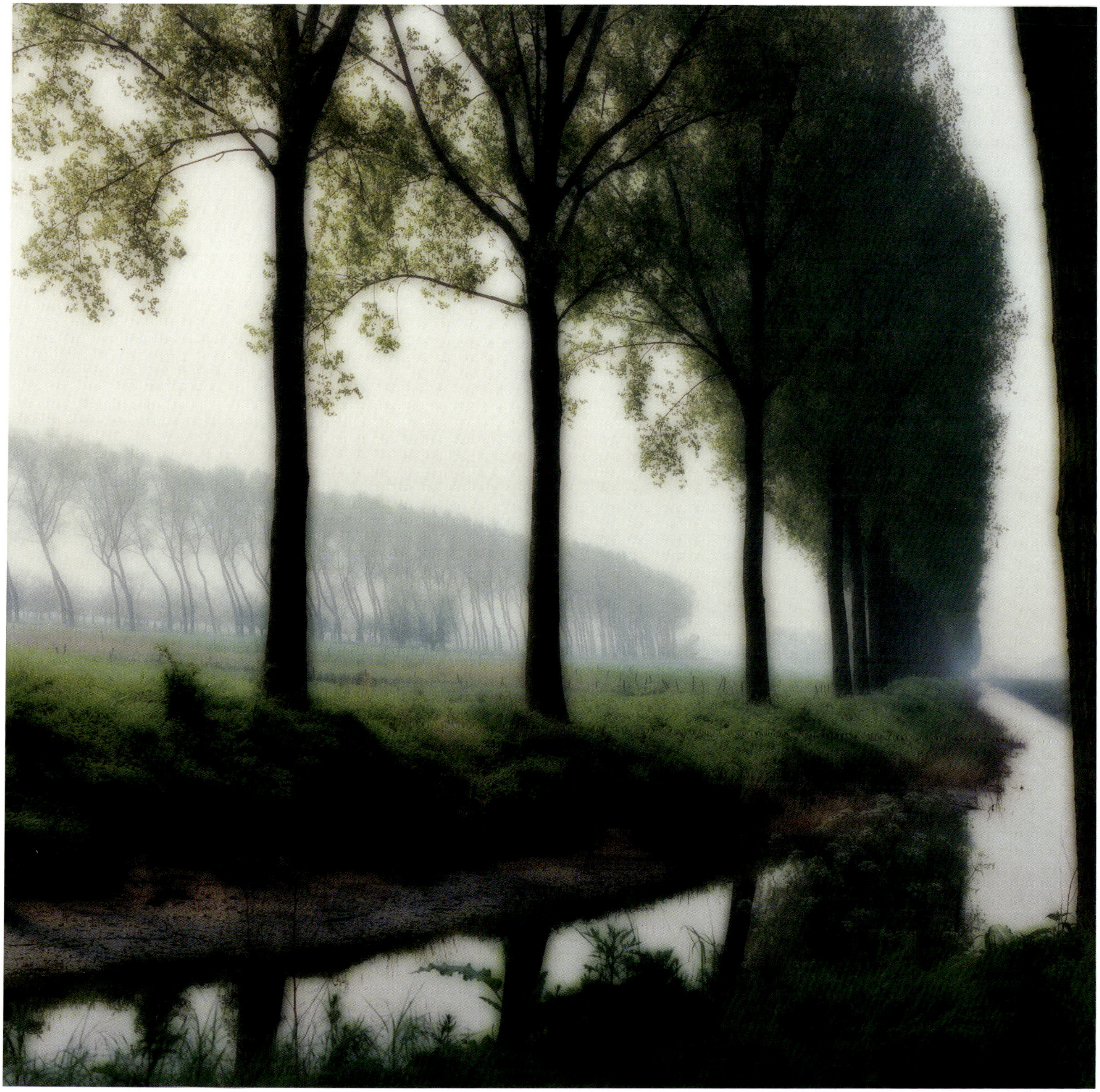

A classic pastoral landscape of the Belgian lowlands, this photograph worked well in black-and-white as well as color. The cows were in no hurry.

Damme, near Bruges, Belgium, 1995

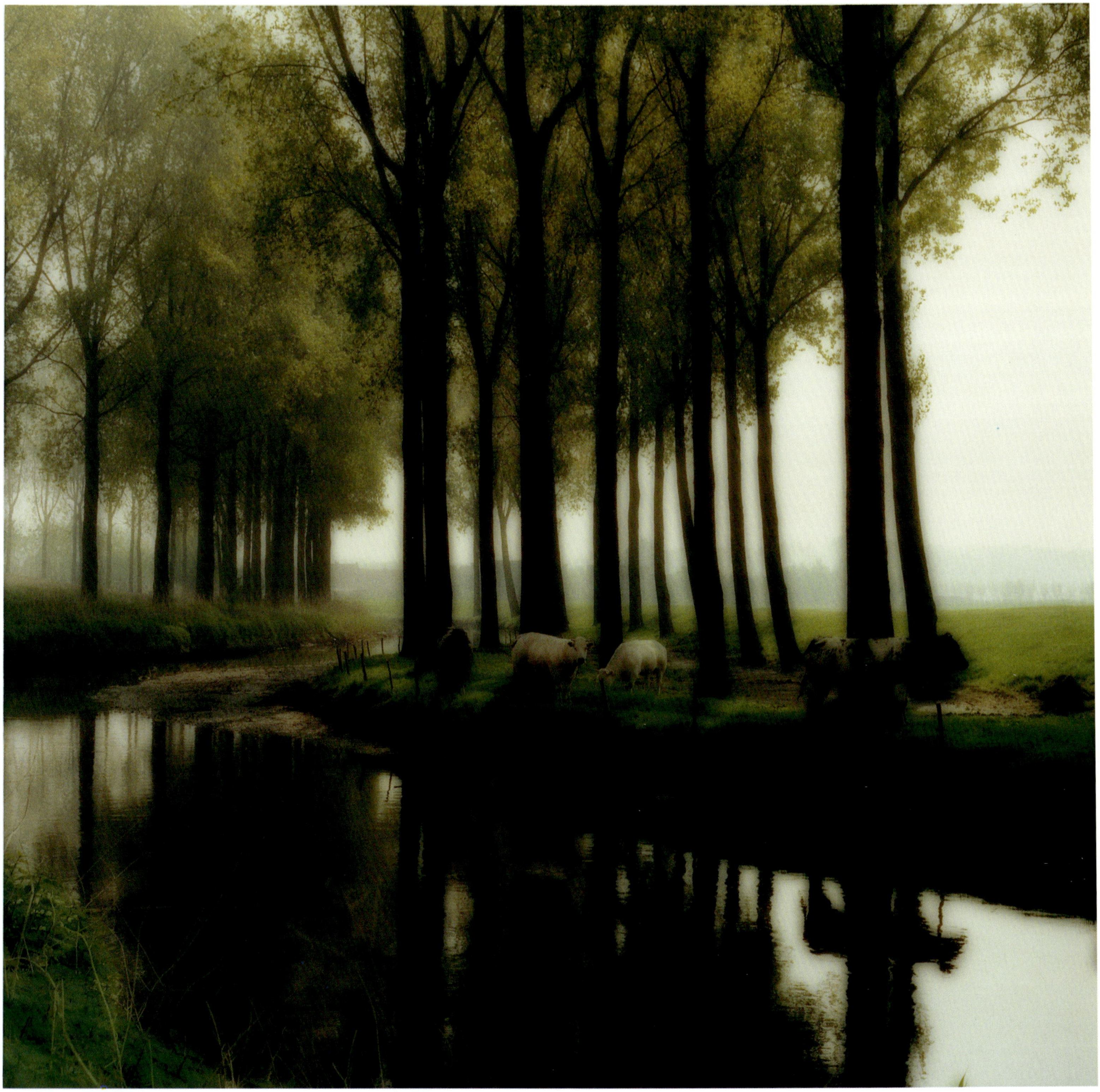

Sluis, the Netherlands, 1995

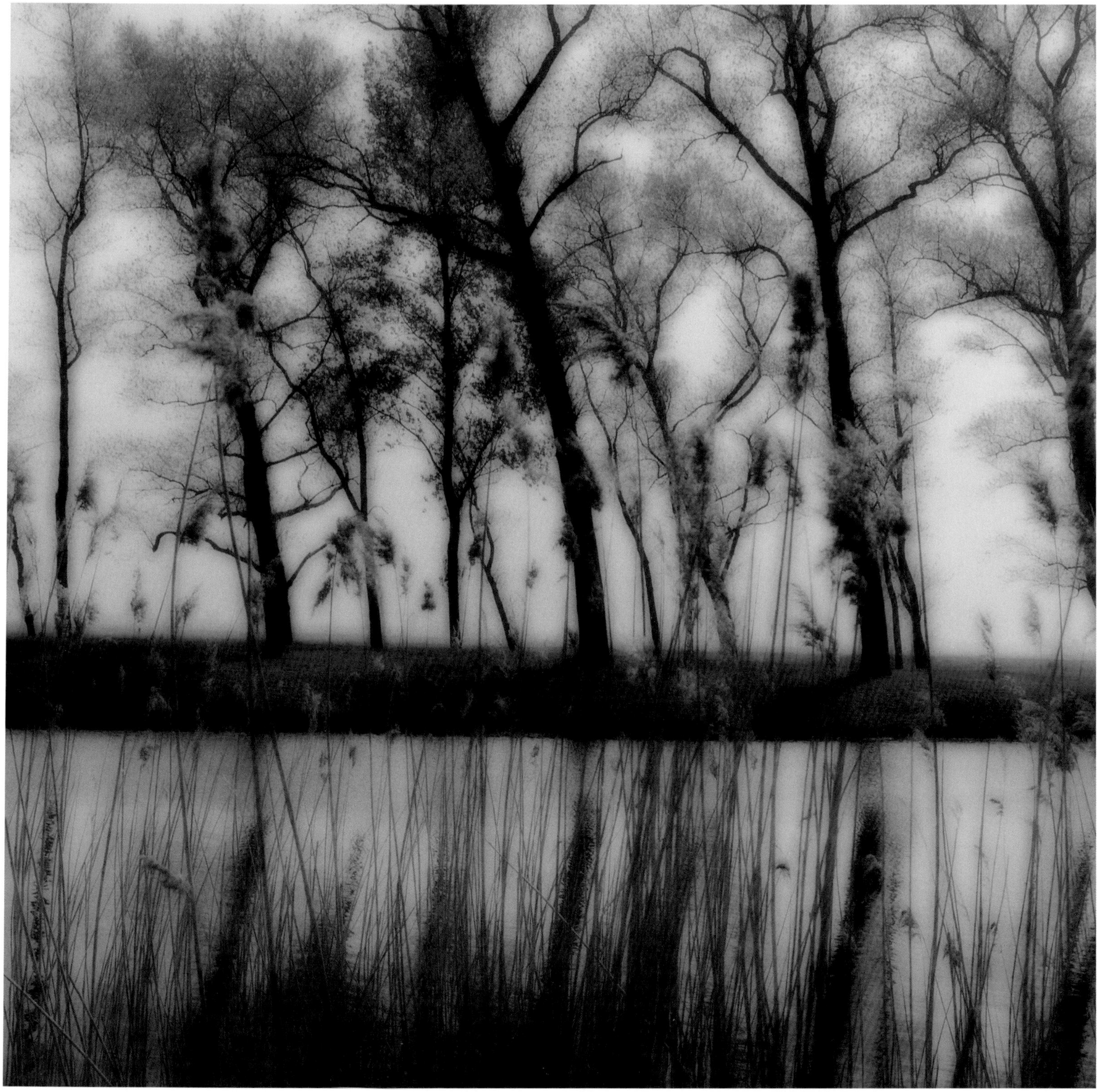

It's like this: for years you dream of going to Andalucia to photograph the olive trees on the hillsides, but when you finally get there, they are déjà vu. Instead, you fall in love with groves of poplar trees on the Granada plains, as if they were there just for you in the pale blue morning light.

Andalucia, Spain, 2002

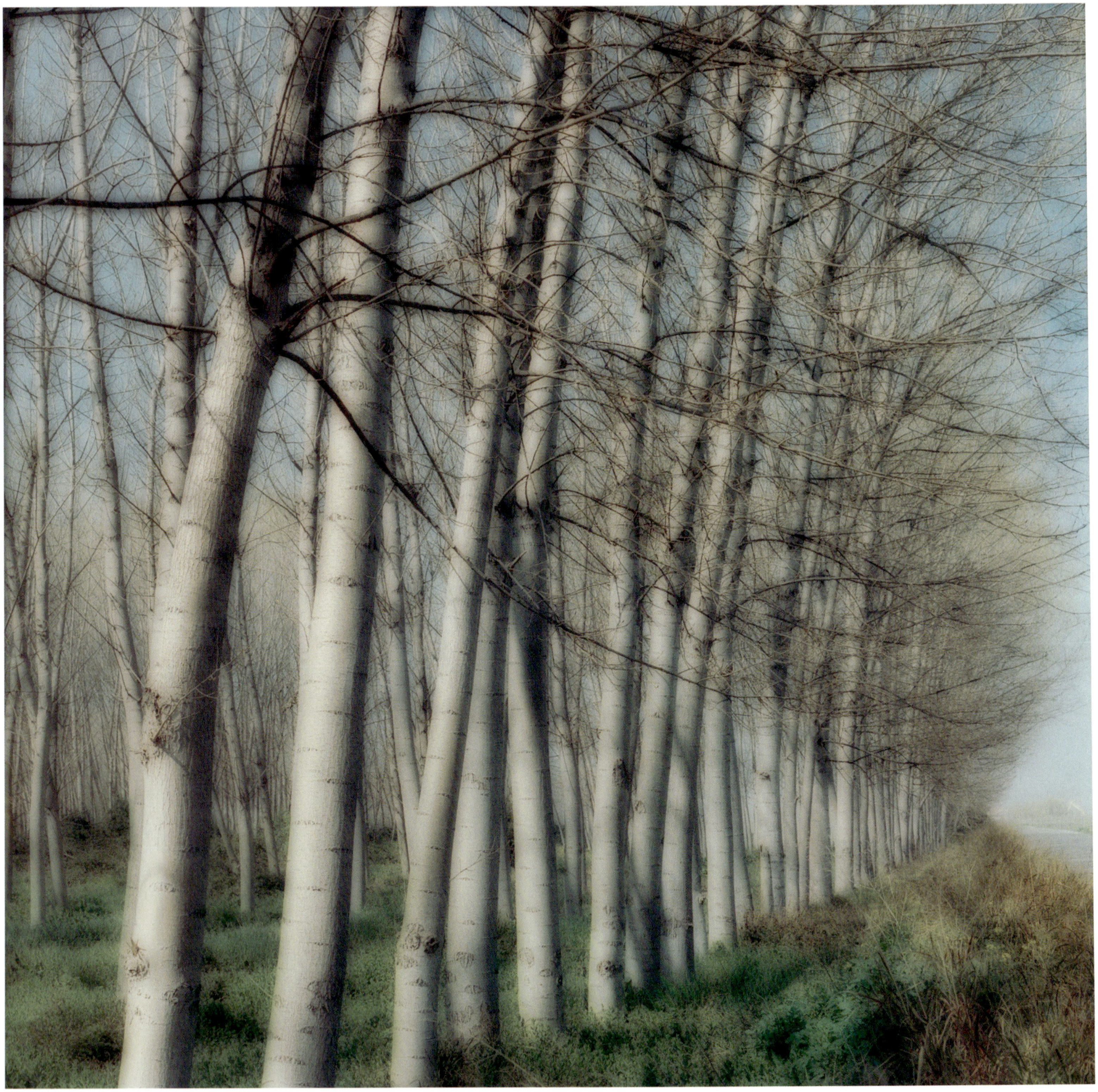

Palacio de Viana, Cordoba, Spain, 2002

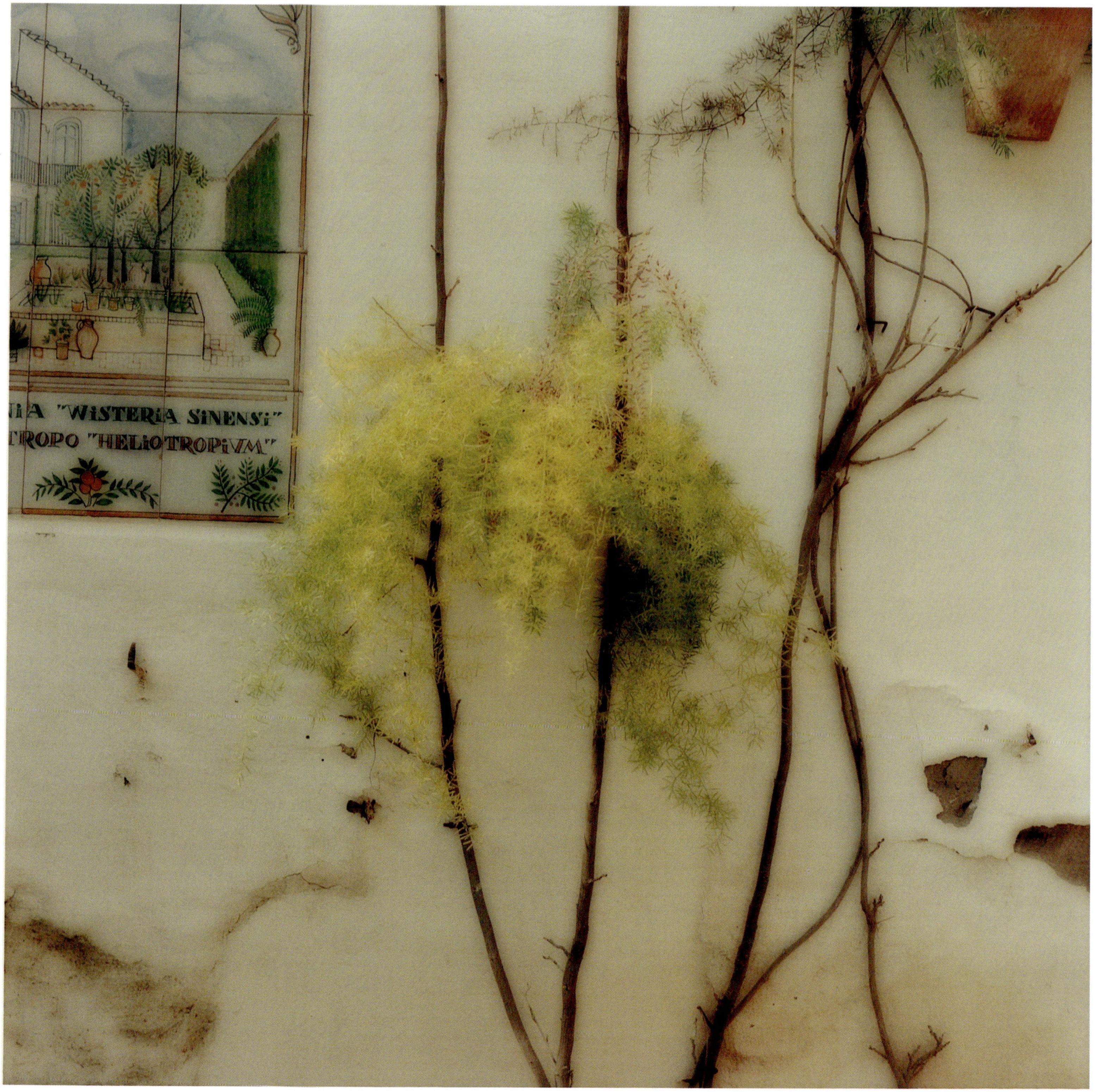

An Italian designer built this Spanish version of Versailles
for the grandson of Louis XIV near Segovia.
The baroque arch seems to have grown out of the forest.

La Granja de San Ildefonso, Segovia, Spain, 2002

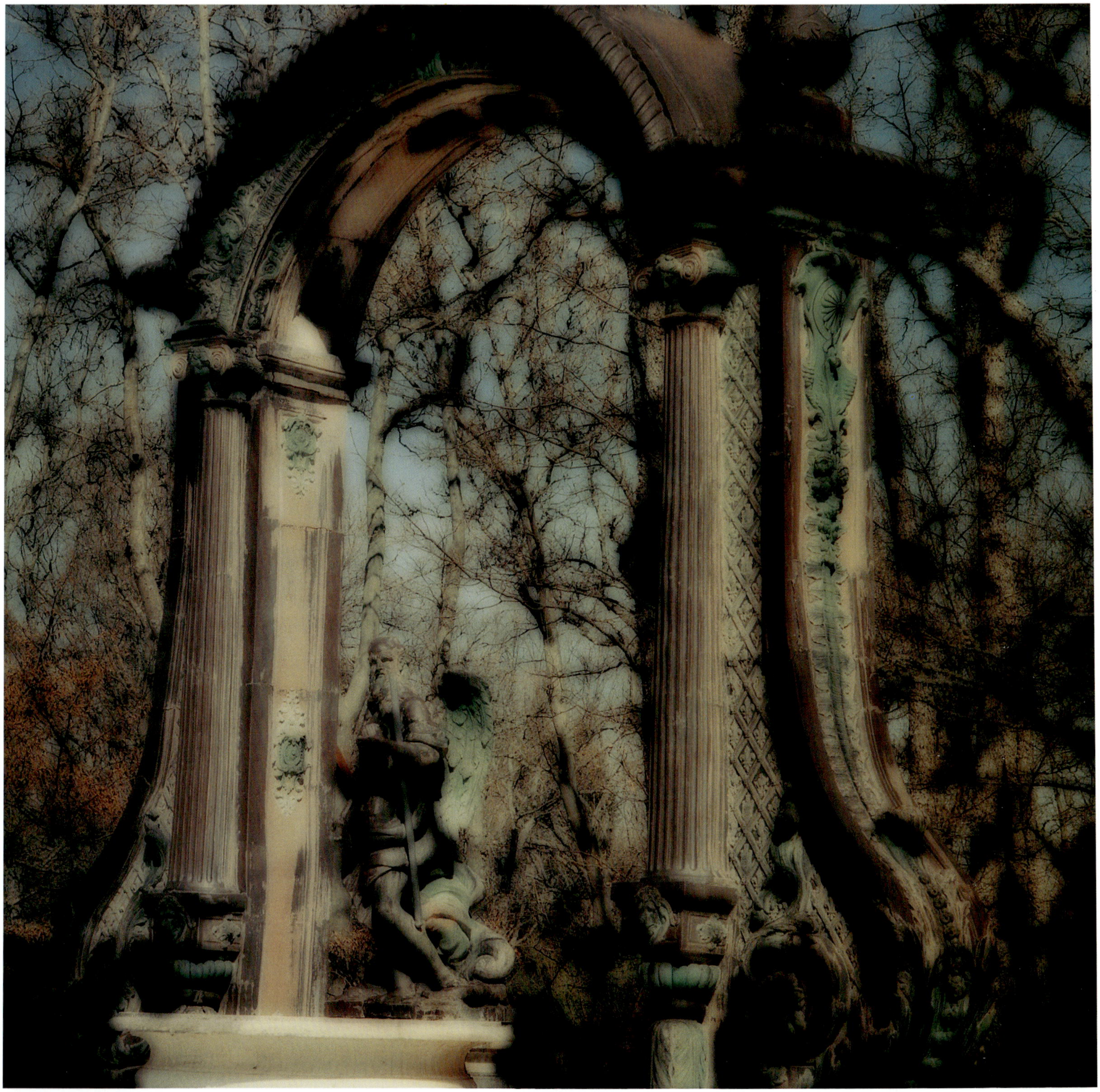

Westerstede, Germany, 1993

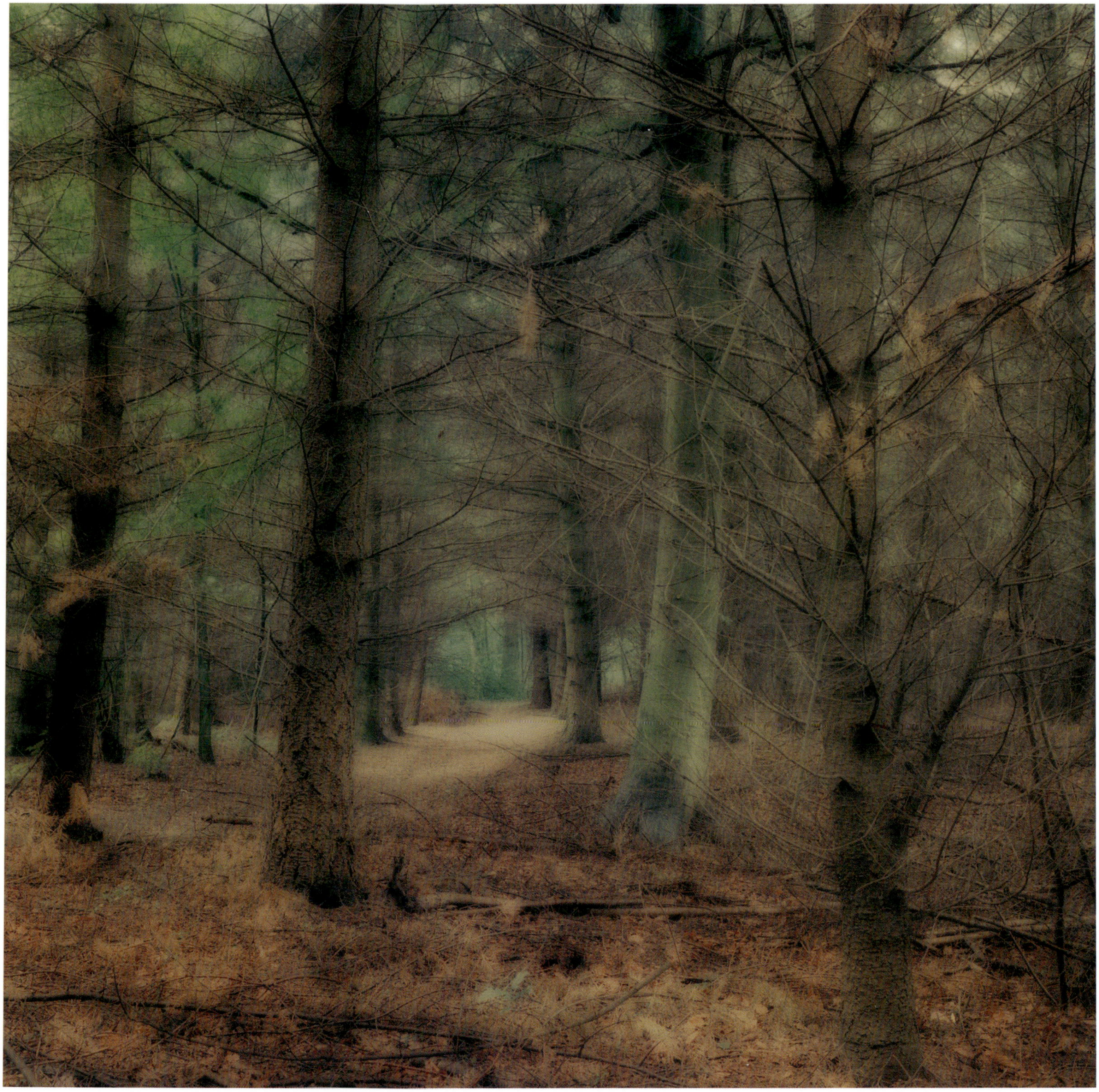

What took me to the Baltic coast of Germany in 1993 was the work of the painter Caspar David Friedrich. His early-nineteenth-century images inspired me to find and photograph those landscapes. The trip was lonely and difficult, but I felt Friedrich's presence on Rügen Island, and his forests have stayed in my memory.

Rügen Island, Germany, 1993

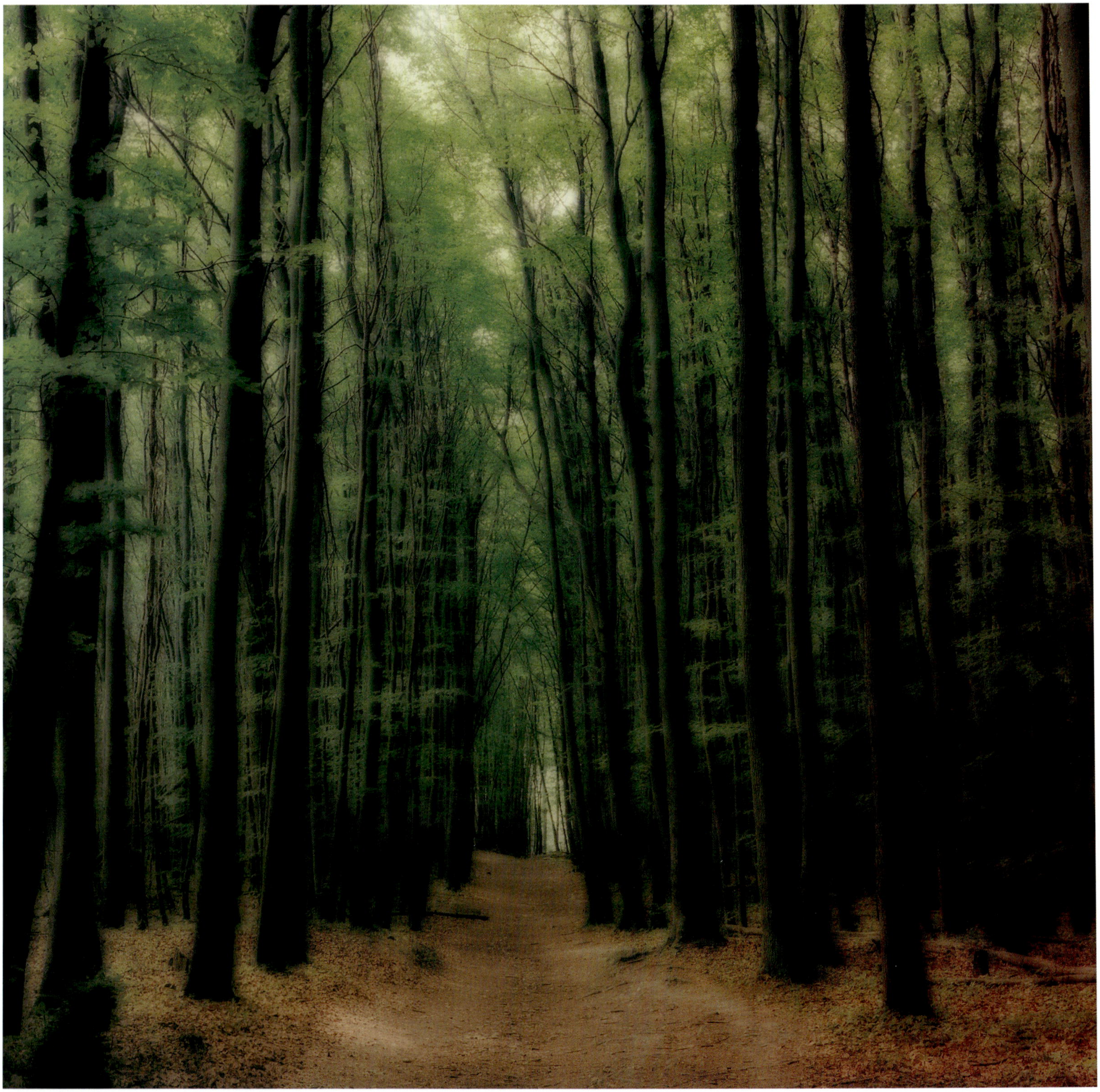

Near the entrance to the villa, a famous garden in the hills outside Florence, there is a tableau of canonical Tuscan beauty — an umbrella pine, a cypress, a wall, and statuary.

Villa Gamberaia, Florence, Italy, 2000

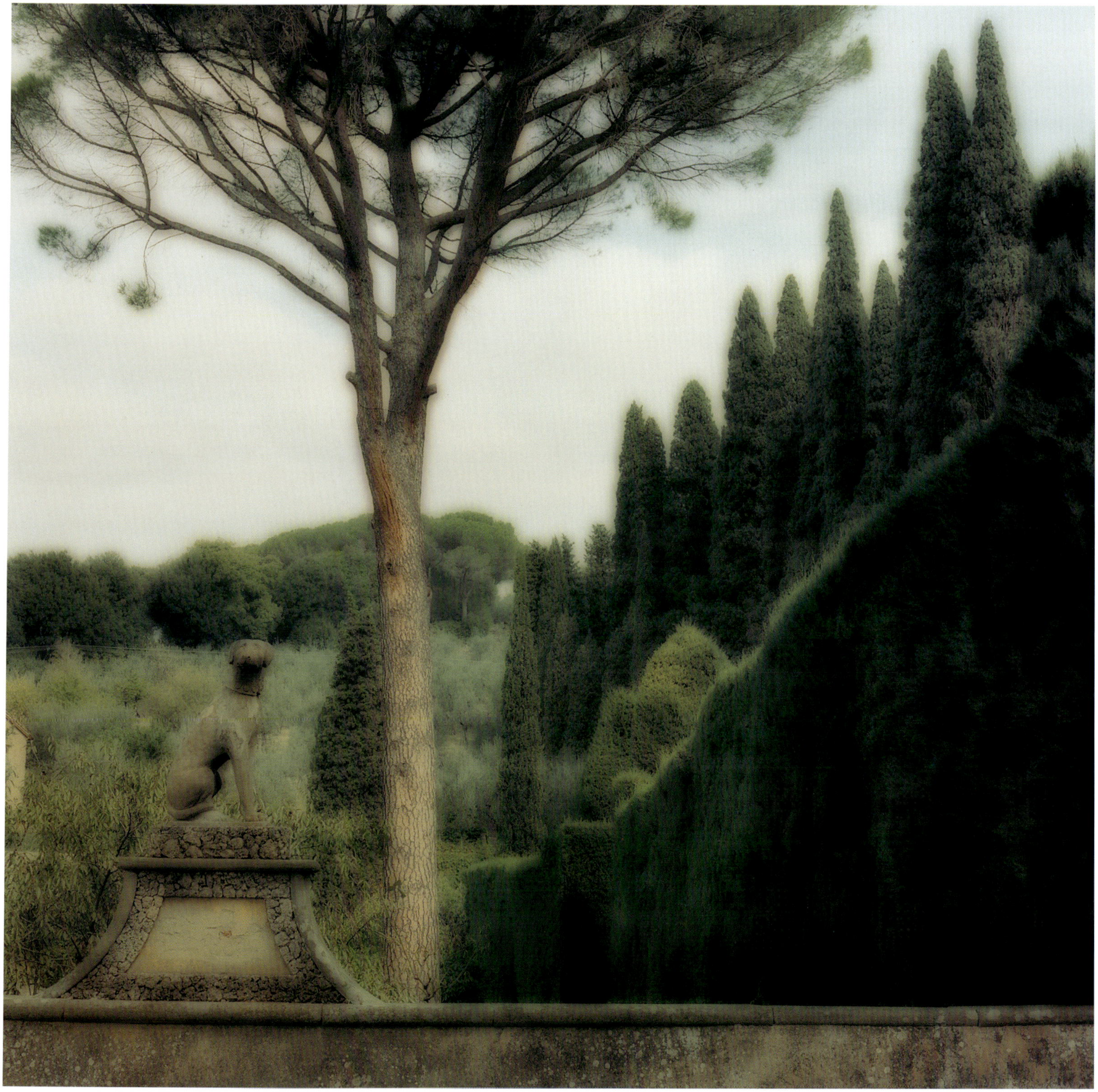

Boboli Gardens, Florence, Italy, 2000

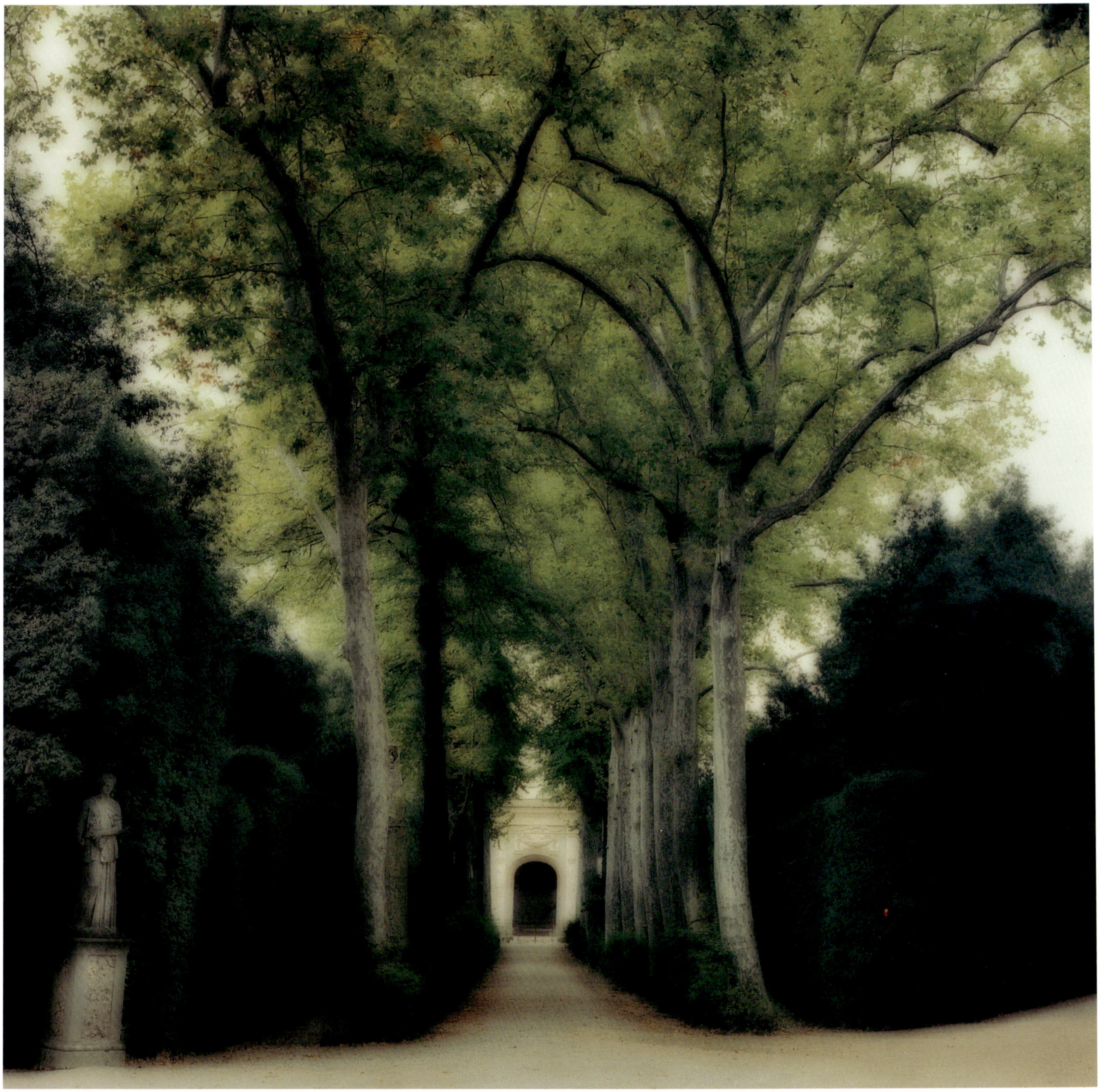

Certosa di Pontignano, Siena, Italy, 2000

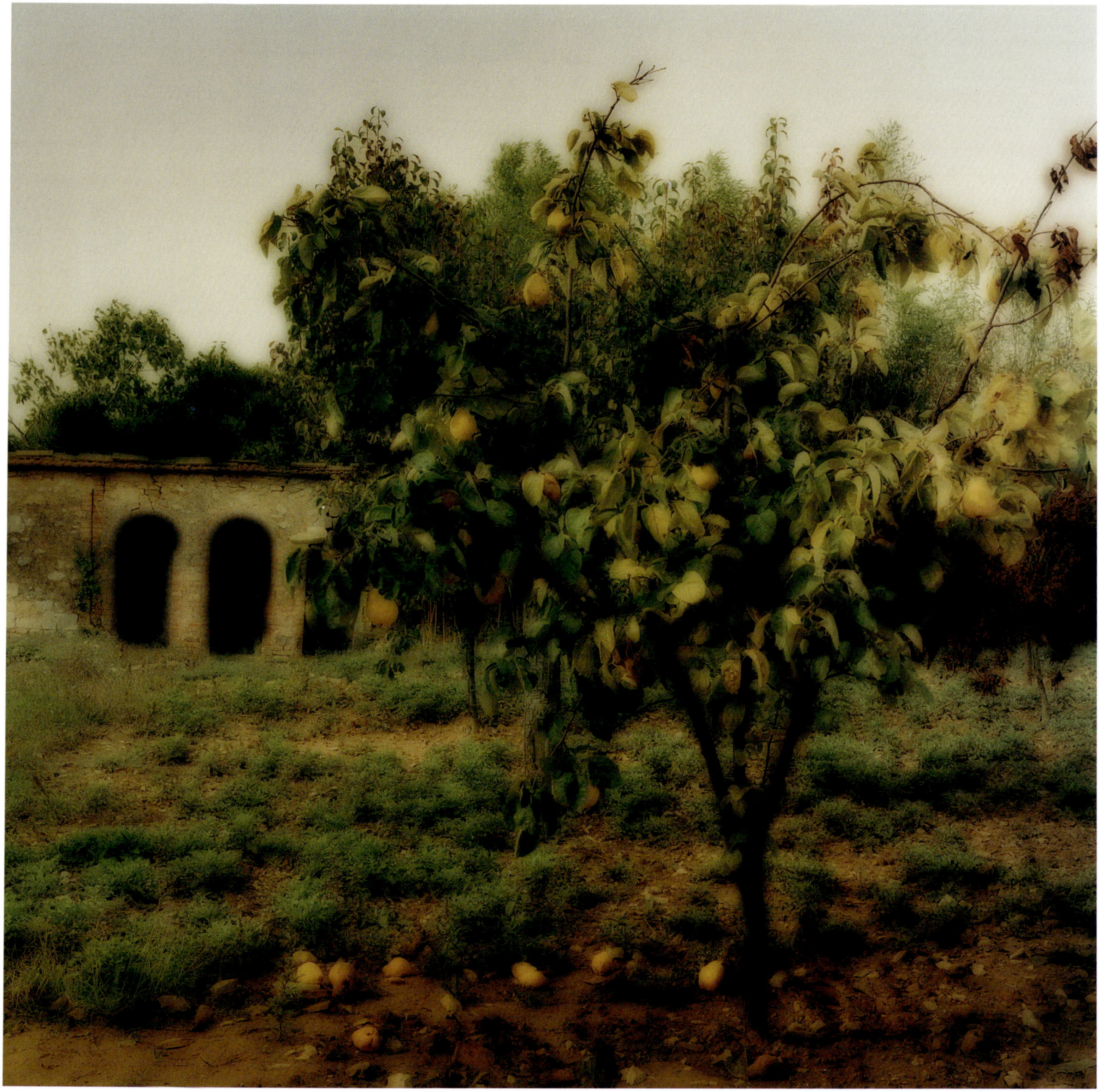

I like the way the vines are trying to escape their confines
in this fourteenth-century monastery garden in the hills above Siena.

Certosa di Pontignano, Siena, Italy, 2000

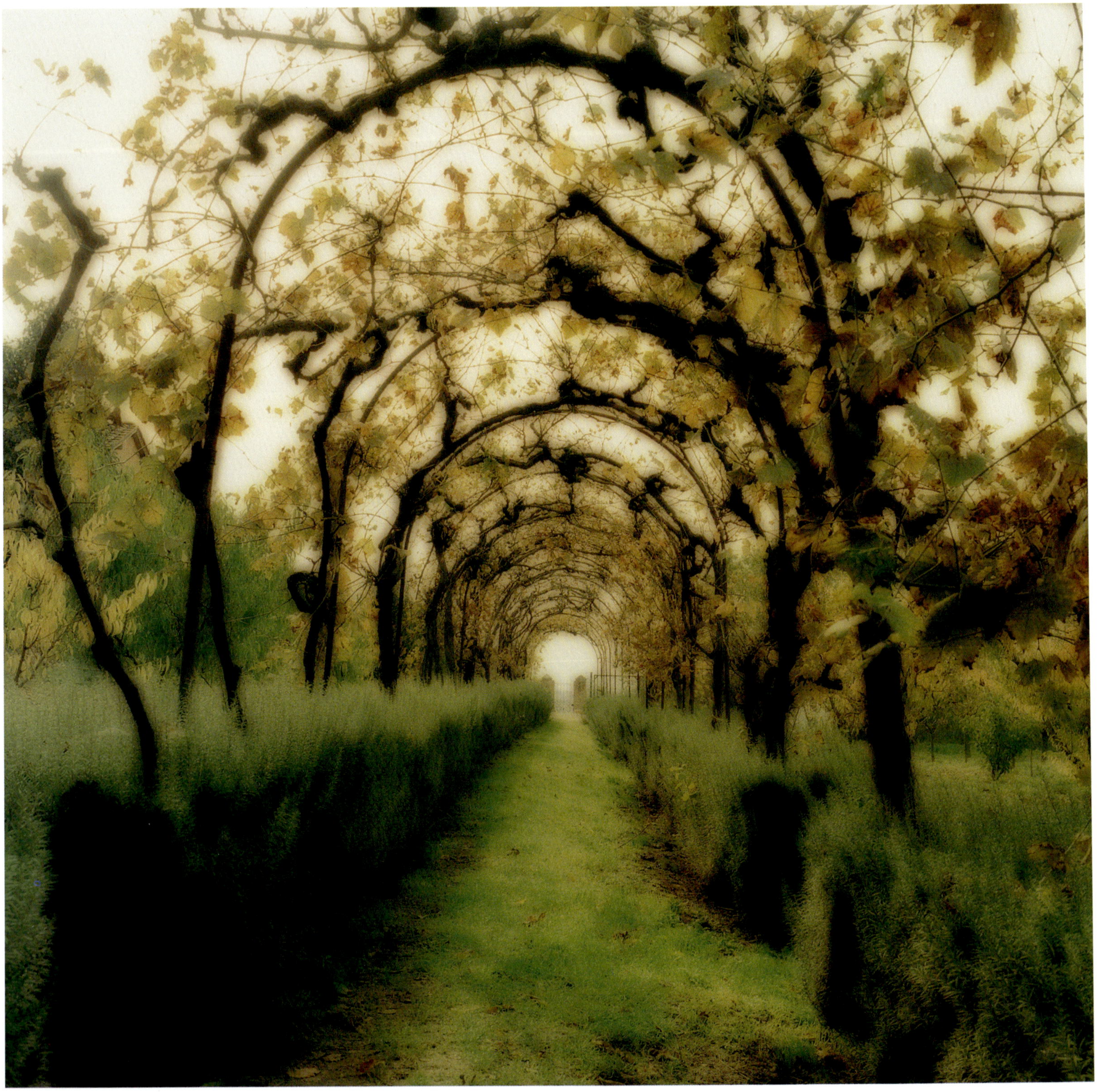

Boboli Gardens, Florence, Italy, 2000

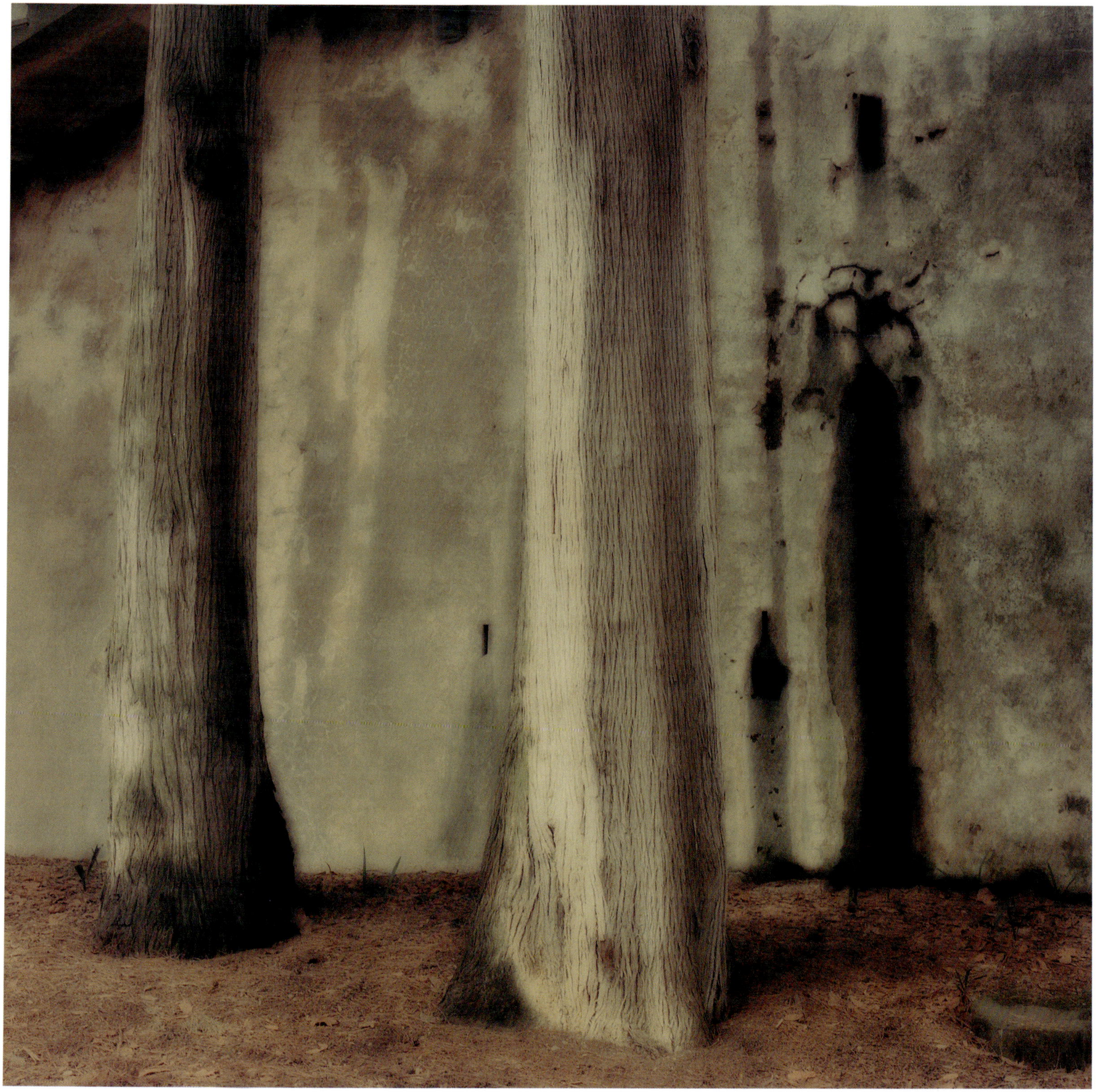

Monticiano, Tuscany, Italy, 2000

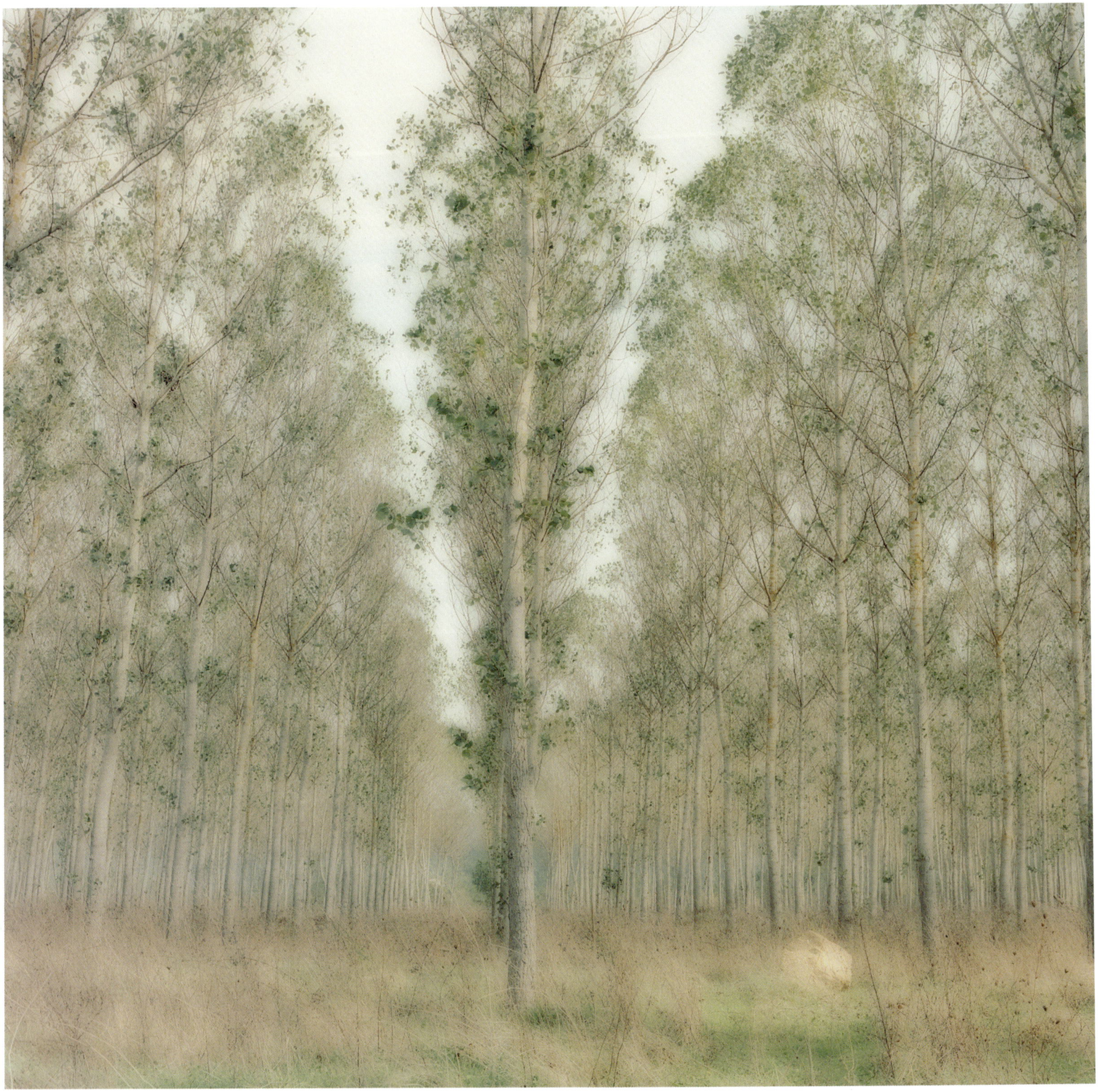

Villa Gamberaia, Florence, Italy, 2000

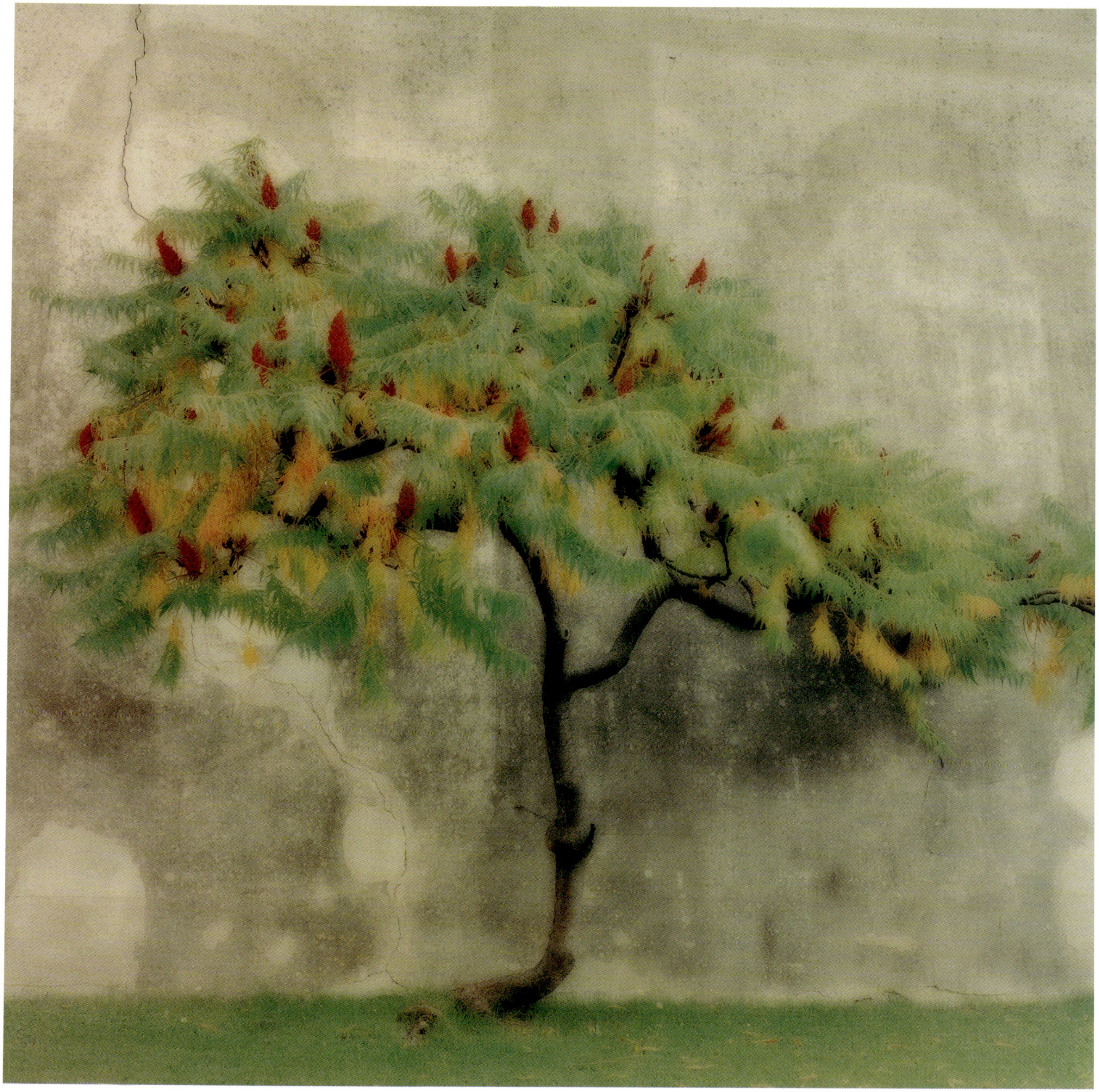

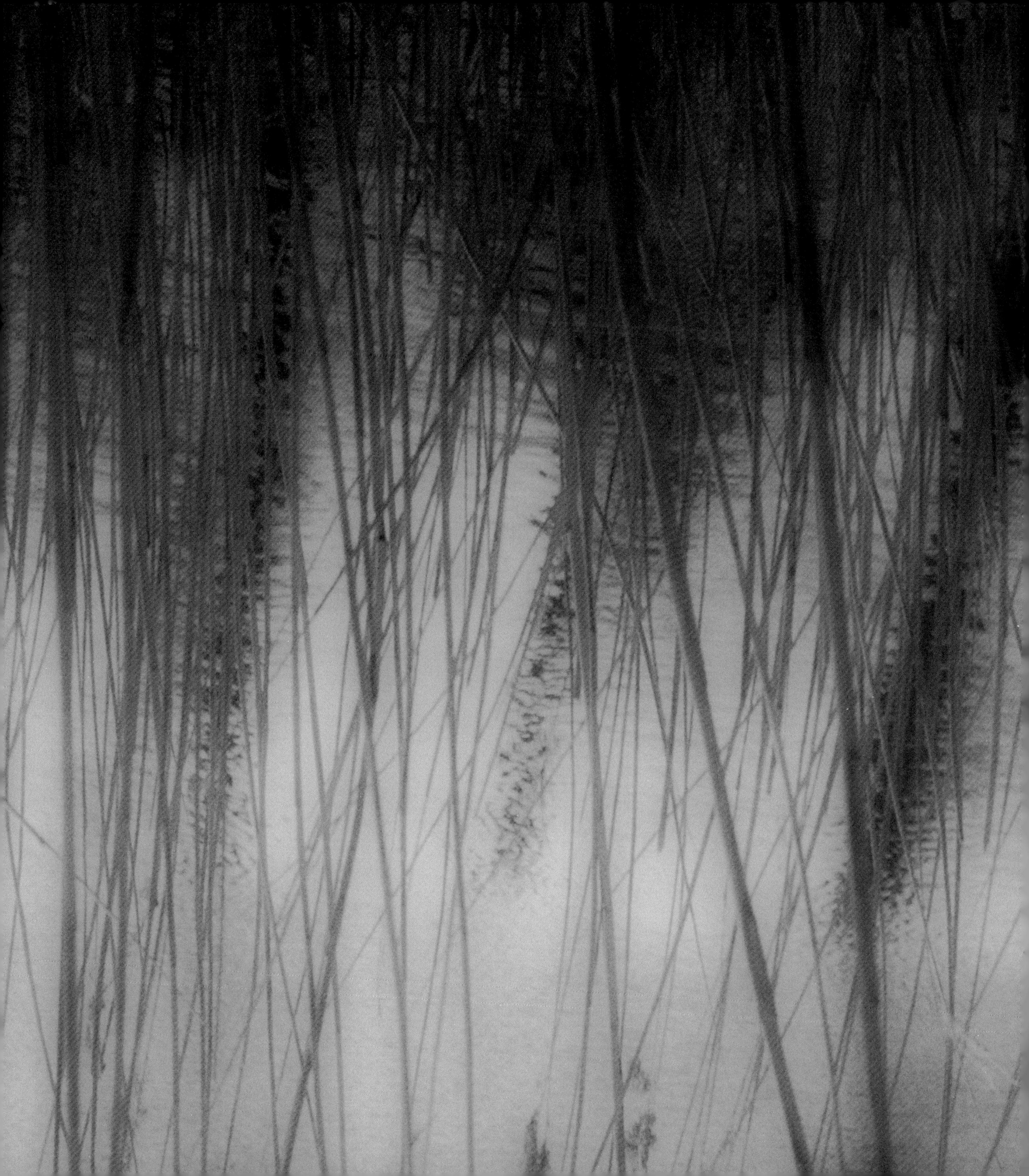

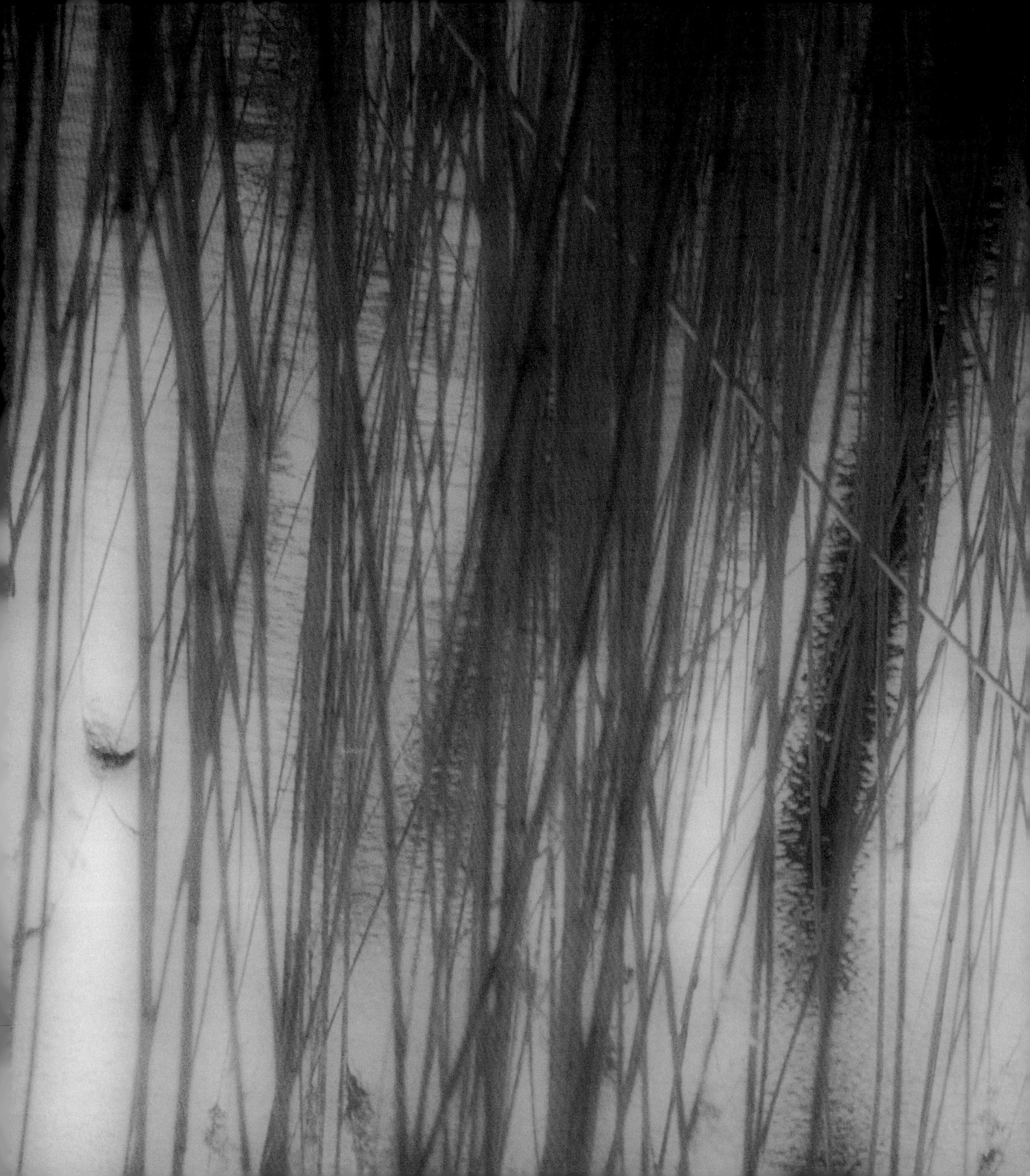

CONDITION OF LIGHT

by Verlyn Klinkenborg

Almost ten years ago, I bought a large black-and-white photograph by Lynn Geesaman called *Dartmoor, England.* It depicts a setting that might have come from Edmund Spenser's *The Faerie Queene*, an irregular row of trees brooding over a hollow lane in rural England. I could almost picture Spenser's gentle knight and his angry steed riding under the arch of those trees, deep within the cover of the lane. Over the years that photograph has hung in several different rooms. Wherever it hangs, it seems to concentrate all the shadows in the house, as though they waited there, latent, until the sun was strong enough to release them at last.

What Geesaman's distinctive technique allows us to see is the potential shadow in the world of her photographs. It's as though she photographed a landscape where hedges and trees refused to throw their shadows but clung to them tightly, an effect that creates a corona of darkness, a crepuscular halo around every object. In the blacks of her black-and-white photographs, there is always a deeper black hiding that makes the world seem more massive and yet more spectral than it really is, as though Geesaman were showing us the perceptual solidity and the quantum uncertainty of the world all at once.

I think we forget what a trope black-and-white photography is, what a brutal substitution it involves, leaching the color out of the

life around us and replacing it with the harmonics of the gray scale. And if there's a trope involved in learning to see the way a black-and-white photographer must, there's an equal trope when a black-and-white photographer, like Geesaman, begins to see in color. It isn't an unlearning, a return to naïve sight. Geesaman's colors don't come from the naturalism of the camera or from the unaided eye. In a sense, she doesn't register the color immediately before her at all. She sees the color that lies on the far side of black-and-white.

Geesaman has said that the strongest influence on her color work is her own body of black-and-white photographs. As a statement about influence, that seems just right, for sooner or later every artist learns to rise from her own ashes. Geesaman's color photographs show the inner scaffolding of her black-and-white photographs. She has returned, in color, to many of the same settings she used in her black-and-white work—in some cases almost the same footprints—and here too, in this newly phosphorescent world, the hedges and trees still cling to their shadows. But she has enlarged the spectrum of those quantum shadows. Where the gray scale ends, a new one begins, a spectrum that encompasses all visible light as well as its unnoticed overtones.

Geesaman has her own technical explanations for how all this works, how in her darkroom she nudges indiscernible information

out of a negative, pushing the colors almost out of register until they evoke the edge of the unnatural. The question isn't how she makes the darkroom do it. It's how, in her own mind, she calibrates the strangeness of these images, how she knows what is too much when it comes to bending color, and how much is not enough. Each of these color images is a leap of faith, for each one reflects the artist's assurance that she has got it right, right not only for her own eye but also for the viewer's eye as well. Shift the colors too far and they spill over into an almost abstract realm. Shift them too little or too clumsily, and you end up with the trite supernatural naturalism of an old hand-painted postcard.

But somewhere in between, somewhere just right, Geesaman shows us what we see, so to speak, only in our peripheral vision, the colors that lie just past the ones we usually take in. In her 1997 photograph of Parc de Sceaux—that astonishing double row of plane trees, one row walking in darkness, the other in light—the colors that emerge in the most luminous parts of the picture seem, at first, only inferentially connected to the everyday spectrum we inhabit. But something in that saturated light stirs an awareness in the viewer. Not of a place or even a time of day. I think of it as an awareness of the condition of light.

What I mean is that even on the most ordinary day, we witness an indescribable crescendo and decrescendo of light, from the

blackness of utter night to the brightness of noon overhead. With the shifting of light goes the shifting of color, day in, day out. Some colors, some intensities of light, return with the regularity of the sun, but others rise and vanish in an instant. We've all seen impossible sunsets. We've all known hours—we call them hours, at any rate—when for some reason the light seemed to till up forgotten emotions within us. There's no living in a world lit daily by that kind of light. We need the solid hues, the dependable colors, to keep us rooted. Whole hillsides of hemlock green are necessary just to go to work. But in the perpetual fluctuation of natural light, those other vestigial colors are always imminent, awaiting just the right shift in conditions to appear. Geesaman's art is to make them appear, to hold them steady for us while we try to get a fix on our emotions, on those feelings that are just as translucent and brief as the atmosphere in that sunlit corridor in the Parc de Sceaux.

One of those emotions I'd describe, simply, as "being in the world," the sudden lifting of all the brain-rubble that buries us and an abrupt, almost shattering awareness of the presence of the world around us. This is the thing, I think, that phenomenologists try to describe. In fact, it's more easily felt than described. I look at the pears on the ground beneath that pear tree at Certosa di Pontignano, and I believe—I believe—that I know what it's like to have them in my immediate foreground. They thrust themselves at

me while lying there in repose. Somehow, they suddenly vouch for my existence. Their solidity, the way the Siennese light models their form, almost floats on the paper's emulsion, like the tulips in the Parc de Bagatelle or the fallen blossoms of the camellia tree on Avery Island.

That suggests what color has given Lynn Geesaman and what she passes on, as feeling, to the viewer. The visceral massiveness of her black-and-white photographs, their shadowy reluctance, means that their weight lies mainly in the background. The perspective they offer the viewer is foreshortened by the gravity of the dark geometries that inhabit Geesaman's black-and-white pictures. But to turn from black-and-white to color, in Geesaman's work, is to watch the foreground emerge, to see it leap at the eye. You find yourself studying the illusion in each of these color photographs, sensing that those Louisiana camellia blossoms are as superficial, as surface-bound, as the brushstrokes on a late canvas by Turner, yet knowing that they define the middle distance.

What these discoveries must have felt like to Geesaman is probably best sensed in the images themselves. She talks about the freedom that color offers her, the escape from rules. Perhaps that freedom is visible here, in her almost contumacious use of color. Sometimes these hues reinforce the inherent formalism of her compositions. But more often they set off small insurrections. If Geesaman's black-and-white photographs give us the potential

shadows of the world, then it's hard to escape the feeling that these color photographs show us the potential luminosity. The red of those tulips in the Parc de Bagatelle takes us to the end of red, and yet it somehow suggests that there is still more red than the paper or the film or the eye itself can contain.

Some artists only reluctantly come to realize that beyond the problems of technique and composition, beyond the mere play of the materials themselves, there lies the task of saying something about what it means to be in the world, to aspire to some conclusions about this inconclusive condition. There is no such reluctance in Lynn Geesaman's work. The photographs say quite explicitly what she means to say, what her conclusions are. It may be hard to put into words just what those conclusions might be. But then almost any emotions worth having are hard to put into words. I can only imagine how much harder it must be to put them into light.

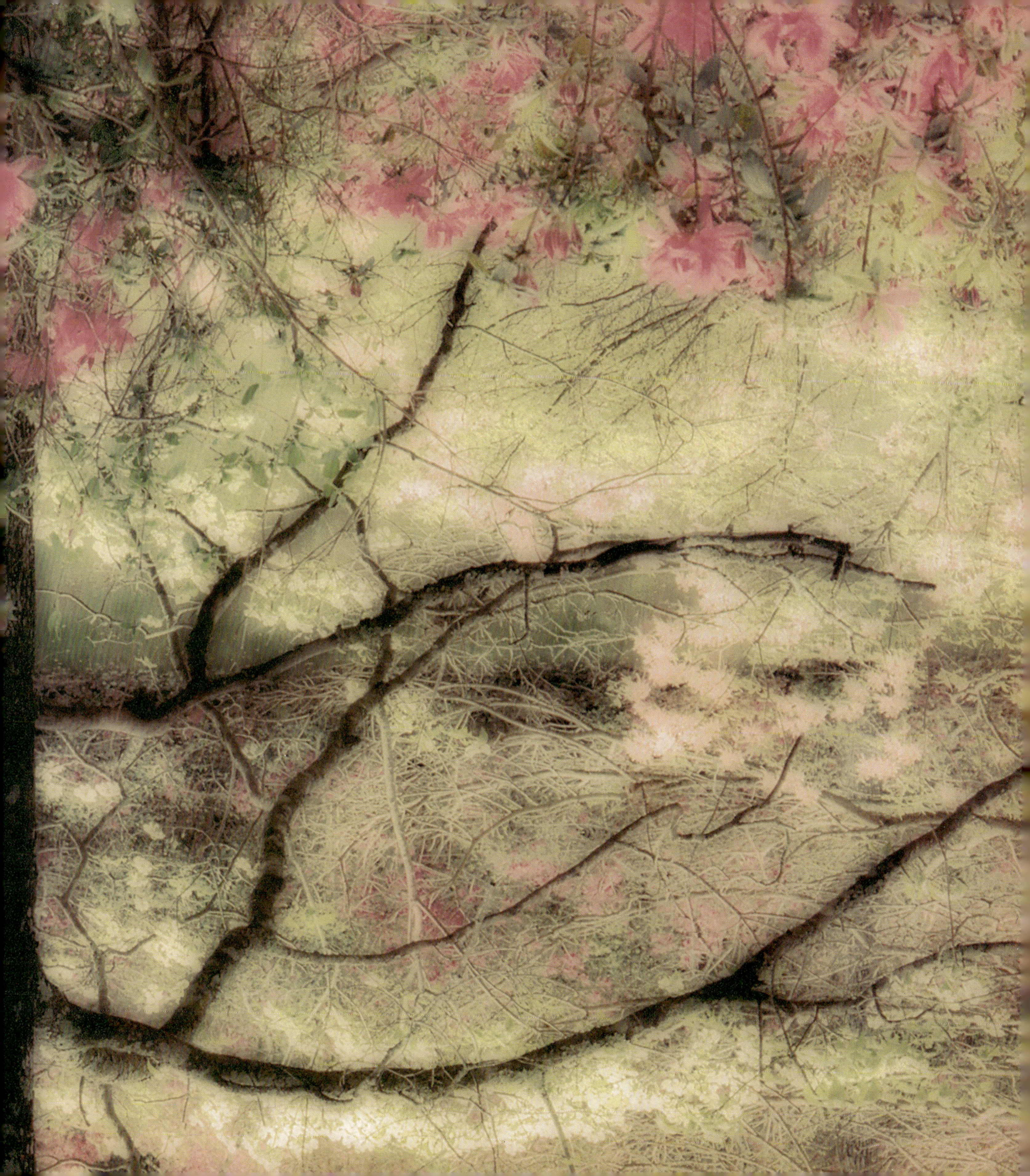

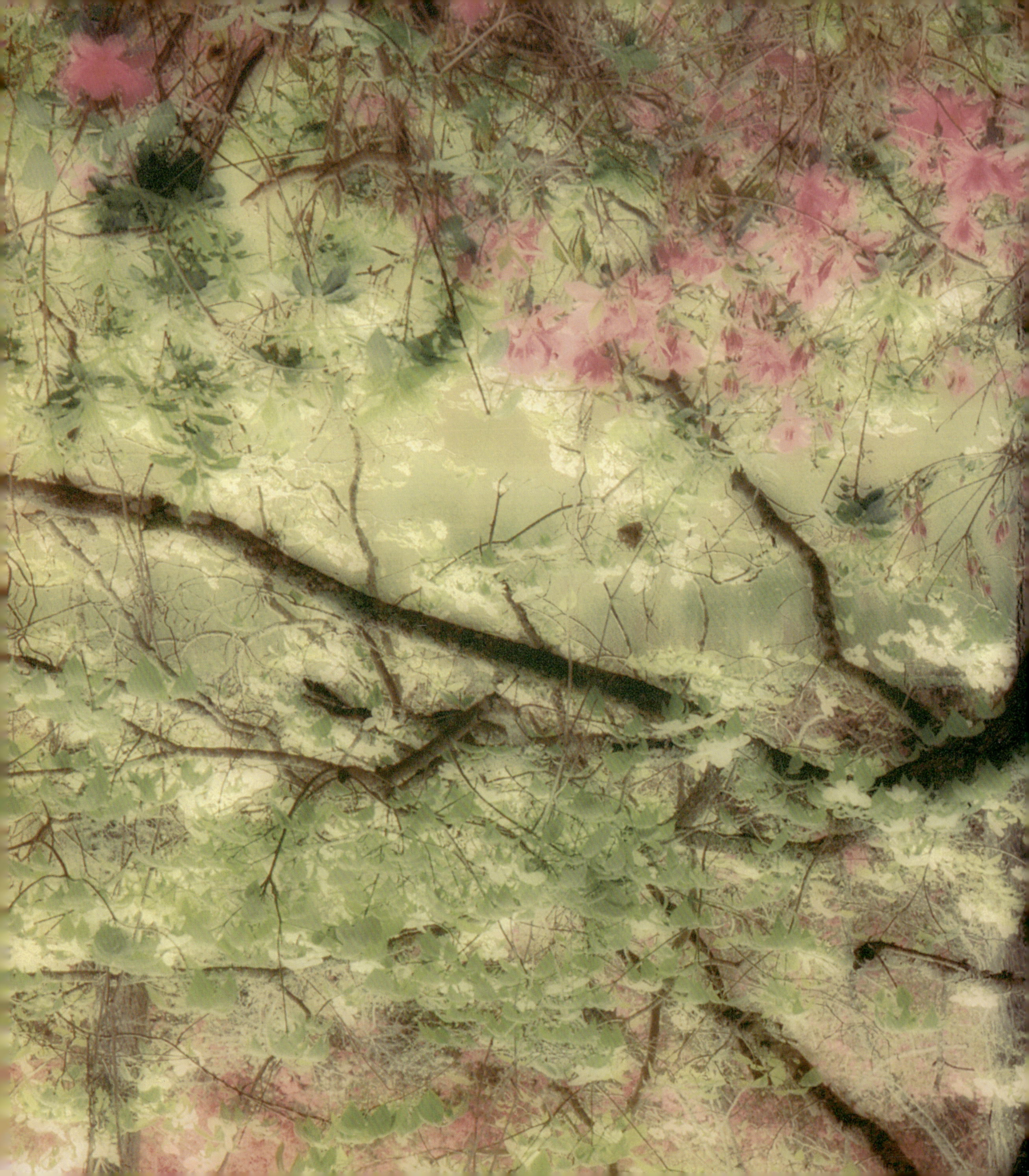

This is a classic pictorialist photograph, but in color. I like the shimmering water and the glow on the sunlit foliage. It is personally interesting to me that I was able to make this picture in an American garden, where similar attempts in the famous English landscape gardens proved futile.

Longwood Gardens, Kennett Square, Pennsylvania, 1994

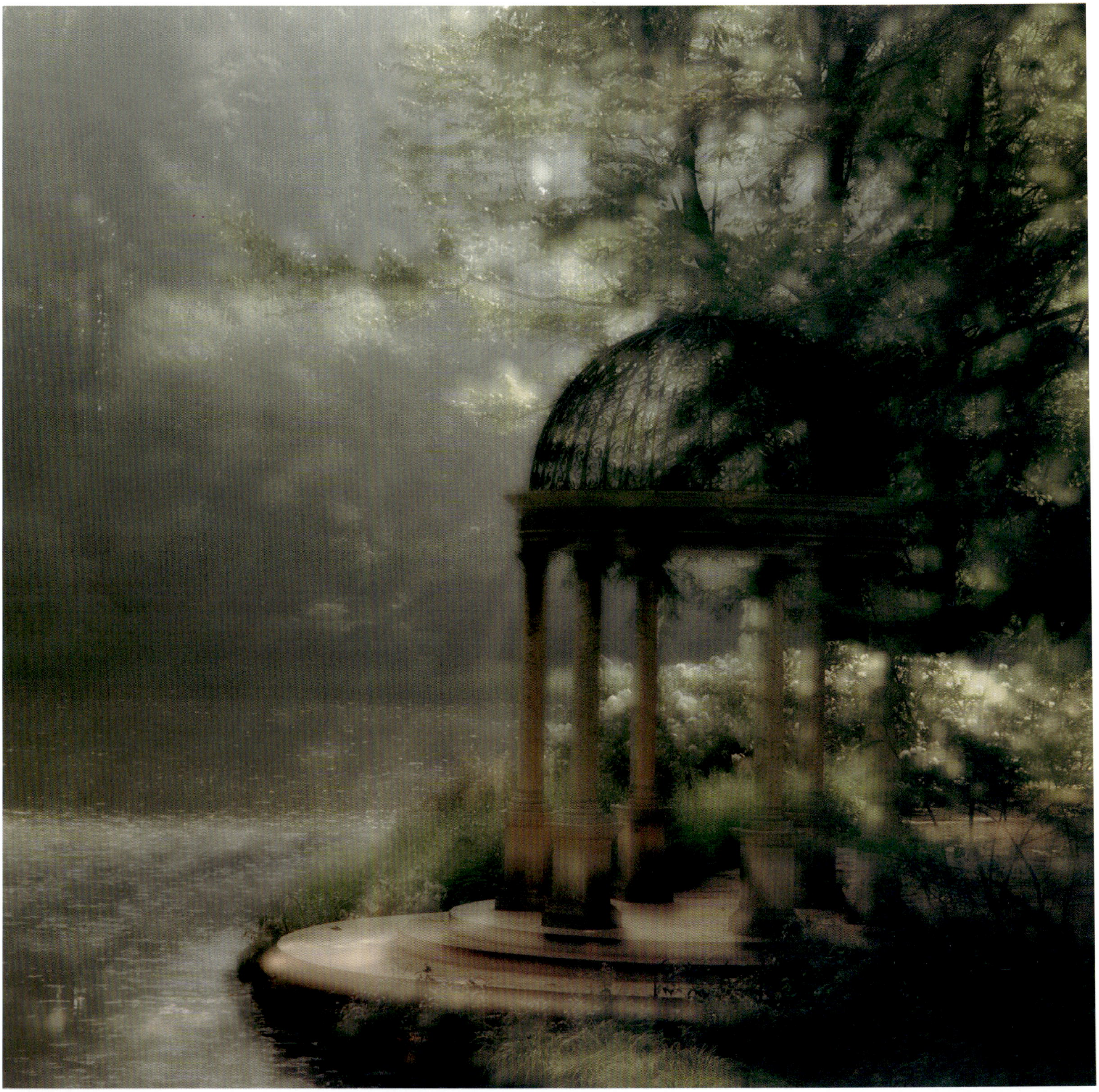

Bernheim Arboretum, Clermont, Kentucky, 1993

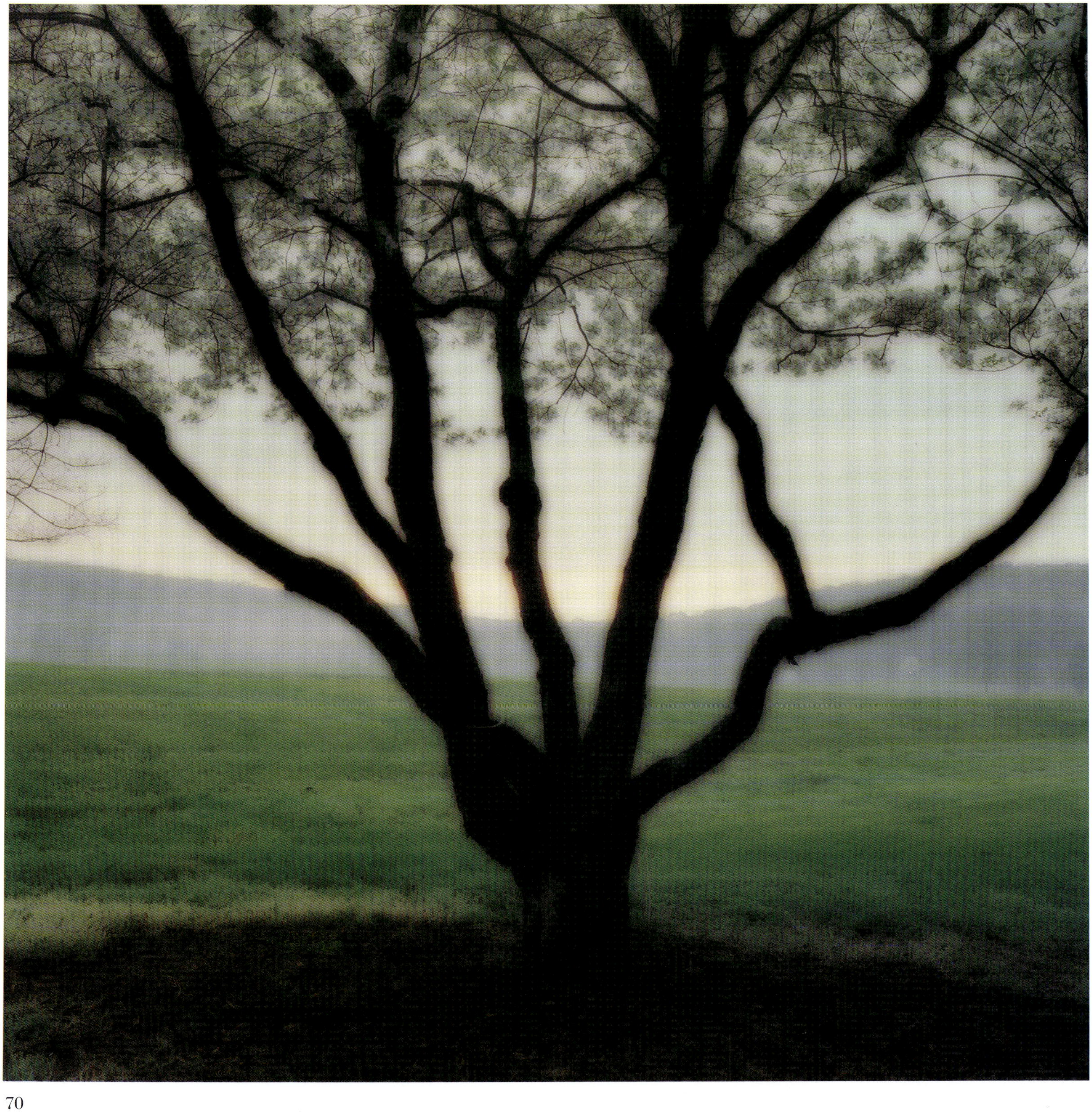

The day was pure springtime, the sky held warm showers, and the graphics were great. This is the site of a legendary Civil War battle and it has a great historical presence.

Antietam National Battlefield, Sharpsburg, Maryland, 1996

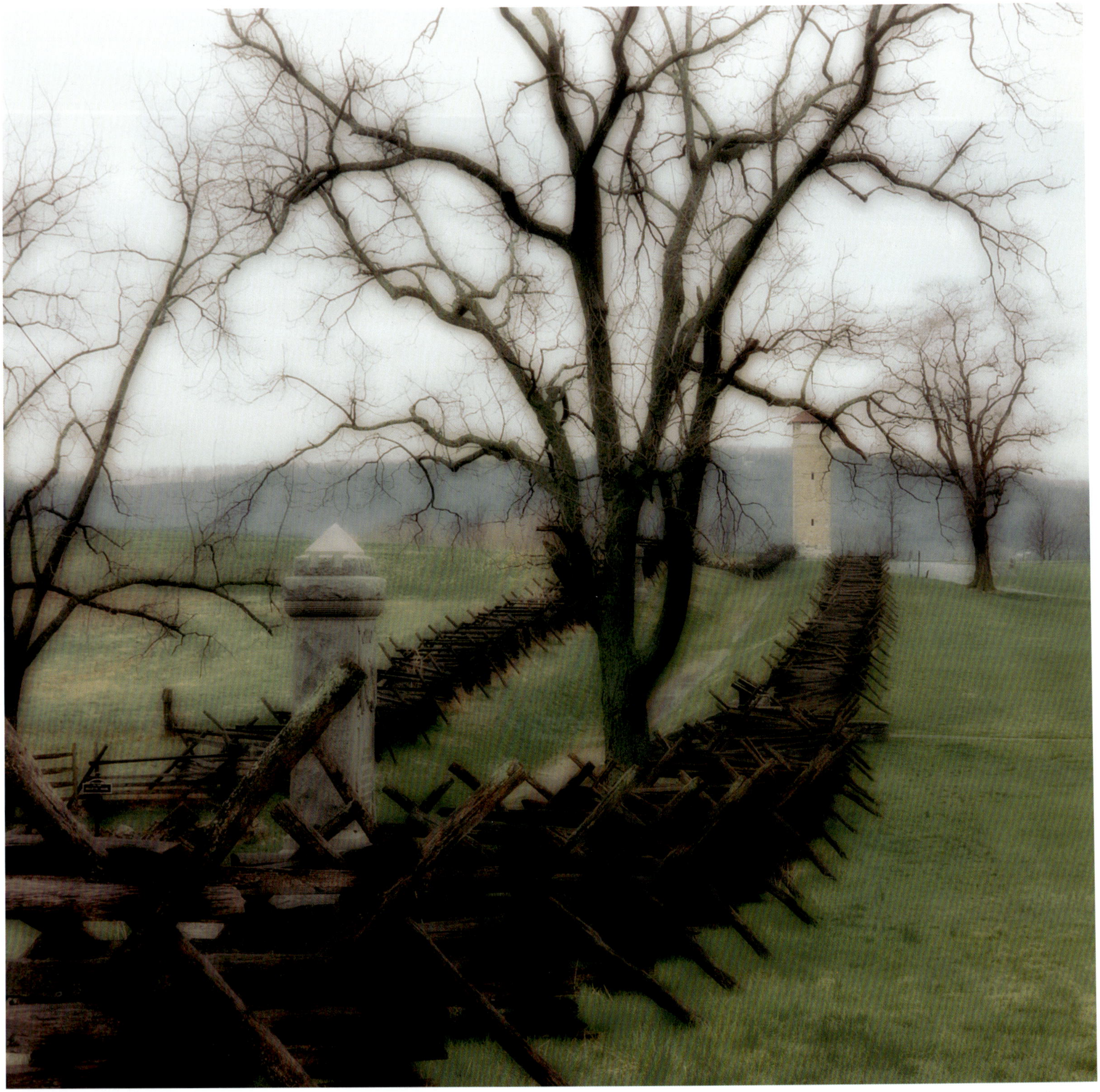

Reflection Riding Arboretum, Chattanooga, Tennessee, 2001

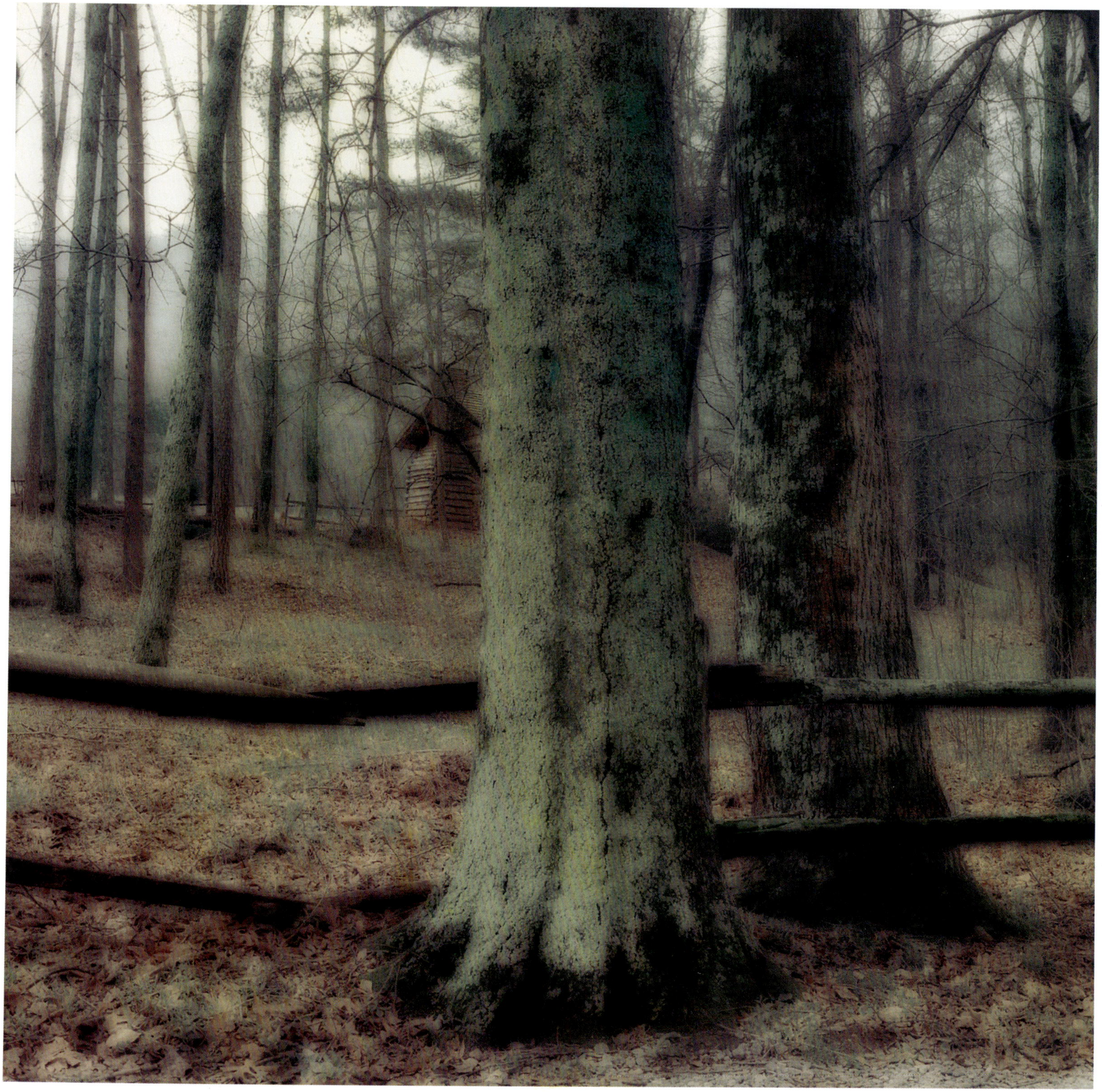

At the foot of Lookout Mountain near Chattanooga, this park resembles an English landscape garden in intent, but is American in essence. I like the conjunction of two different shades of green around the curve, and the old leaves fluttering in wind and rain.

Reflection Riding Arboretum, Chattanooga, Tennessee, 2001

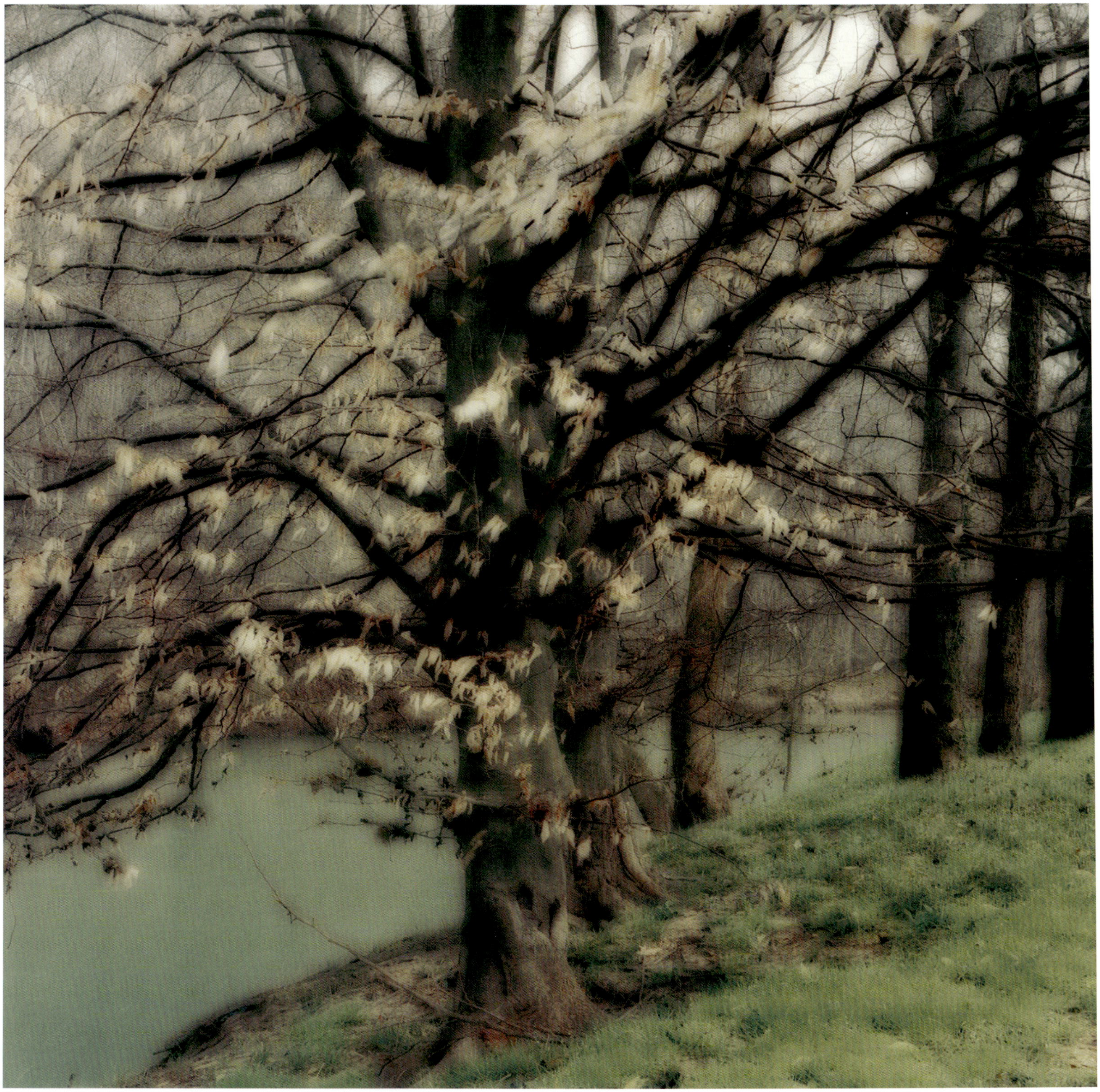

With the help of fog and algae, this forest close-up turned pink and turquoise.
The old leaves could be exotic blooms on oriental branches.
It was all pure chance.

Hot Springs, Arkansas, 1994

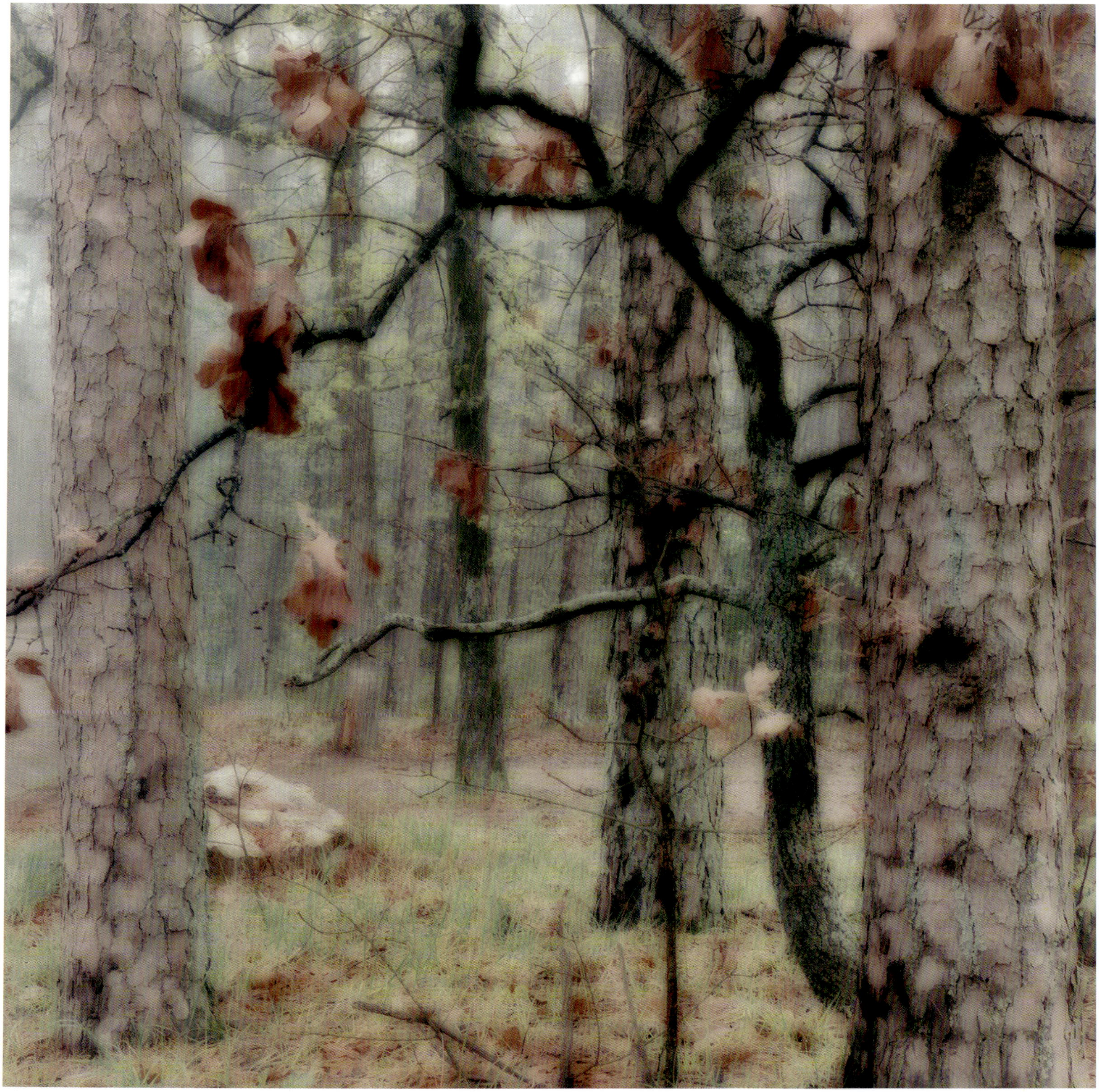

Pea Ridge National Military Park, Pea Ridge, Arkansas, 1994

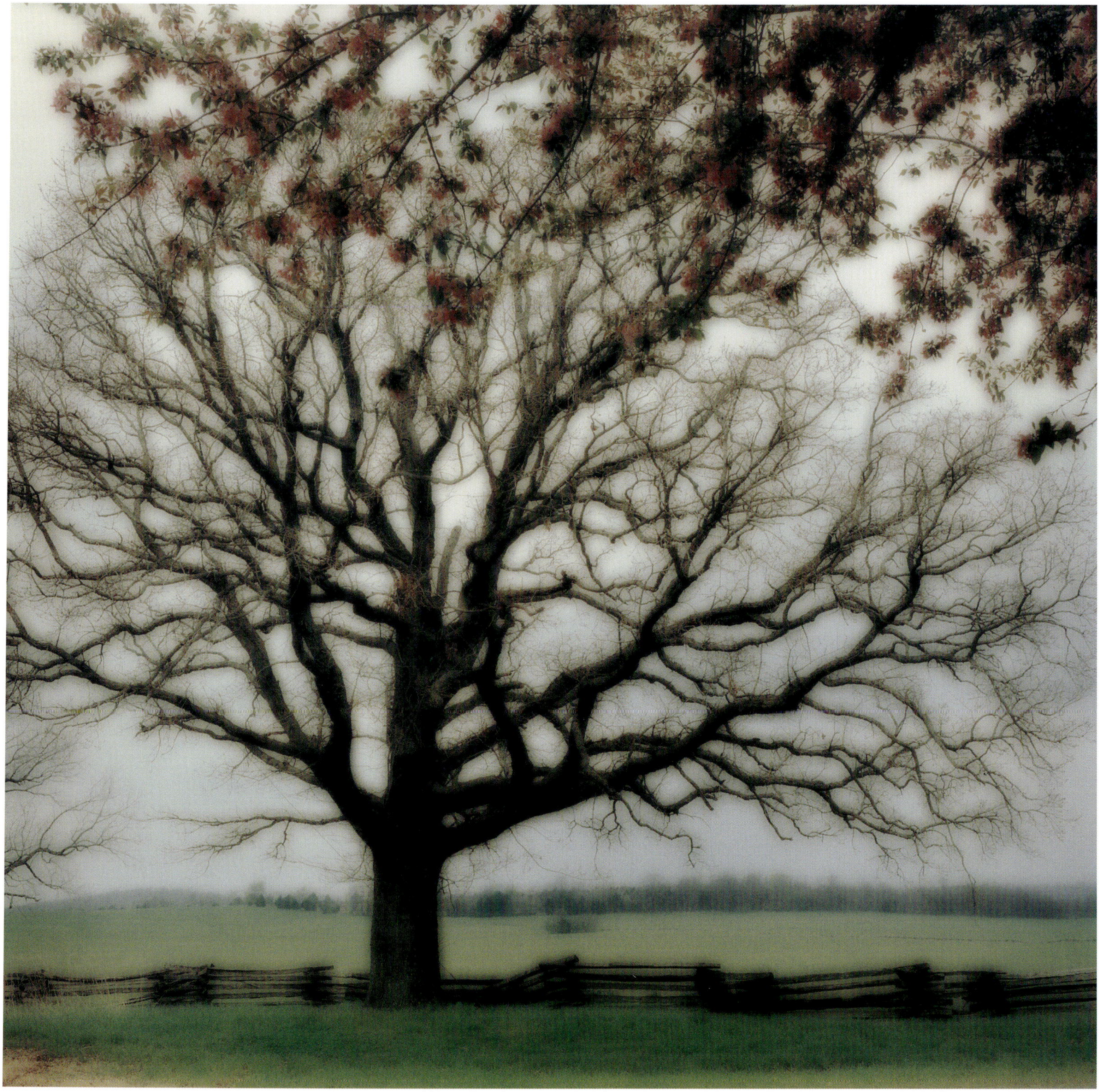

Pea Ridge National Military Park, Pea Ridge, Arkansas, 1994

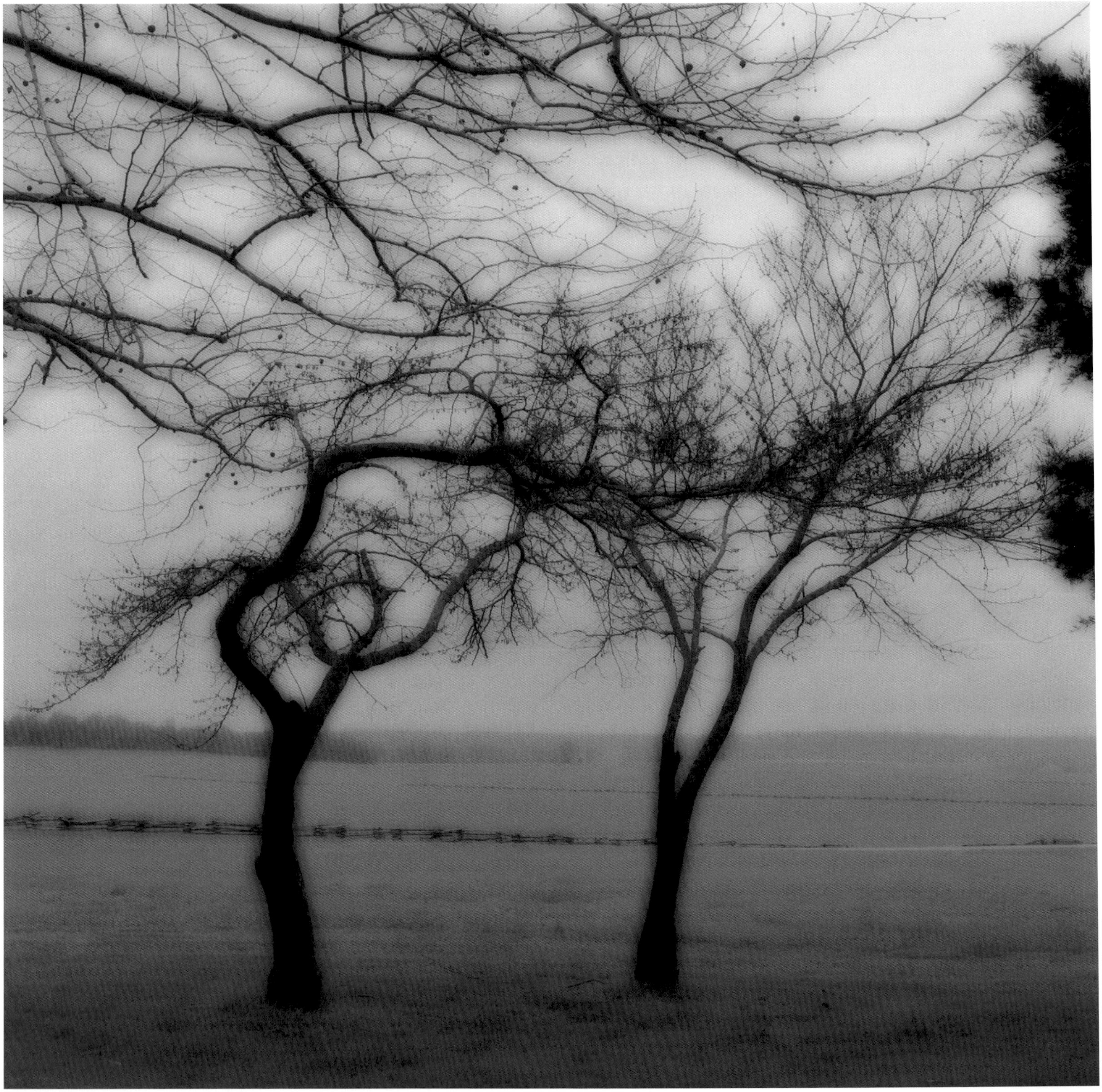

Hot Springs, Arkansas, 1994

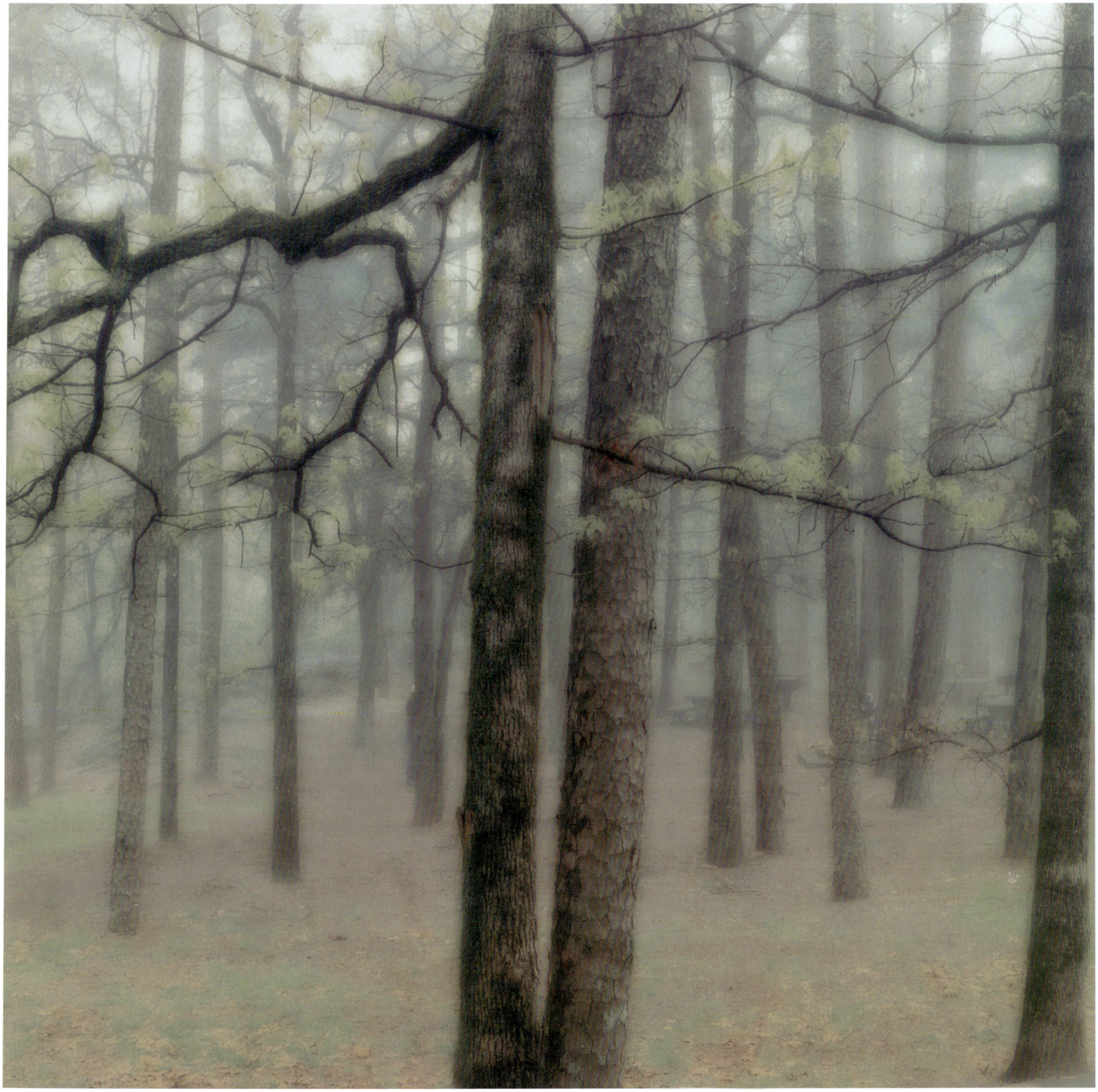

Pale and painterly, the tree was emerging from fog into morning sun. My favorite part of the image is the trunk and the pastel area behind it, with the rim of the lawn reflecting a pale blue cast. The Bernheim Arboretum was originally designed by the Frederick Law Olmsted firm in 1931.

Bernheim Arboretum, Clermont, Kentucky, 1999

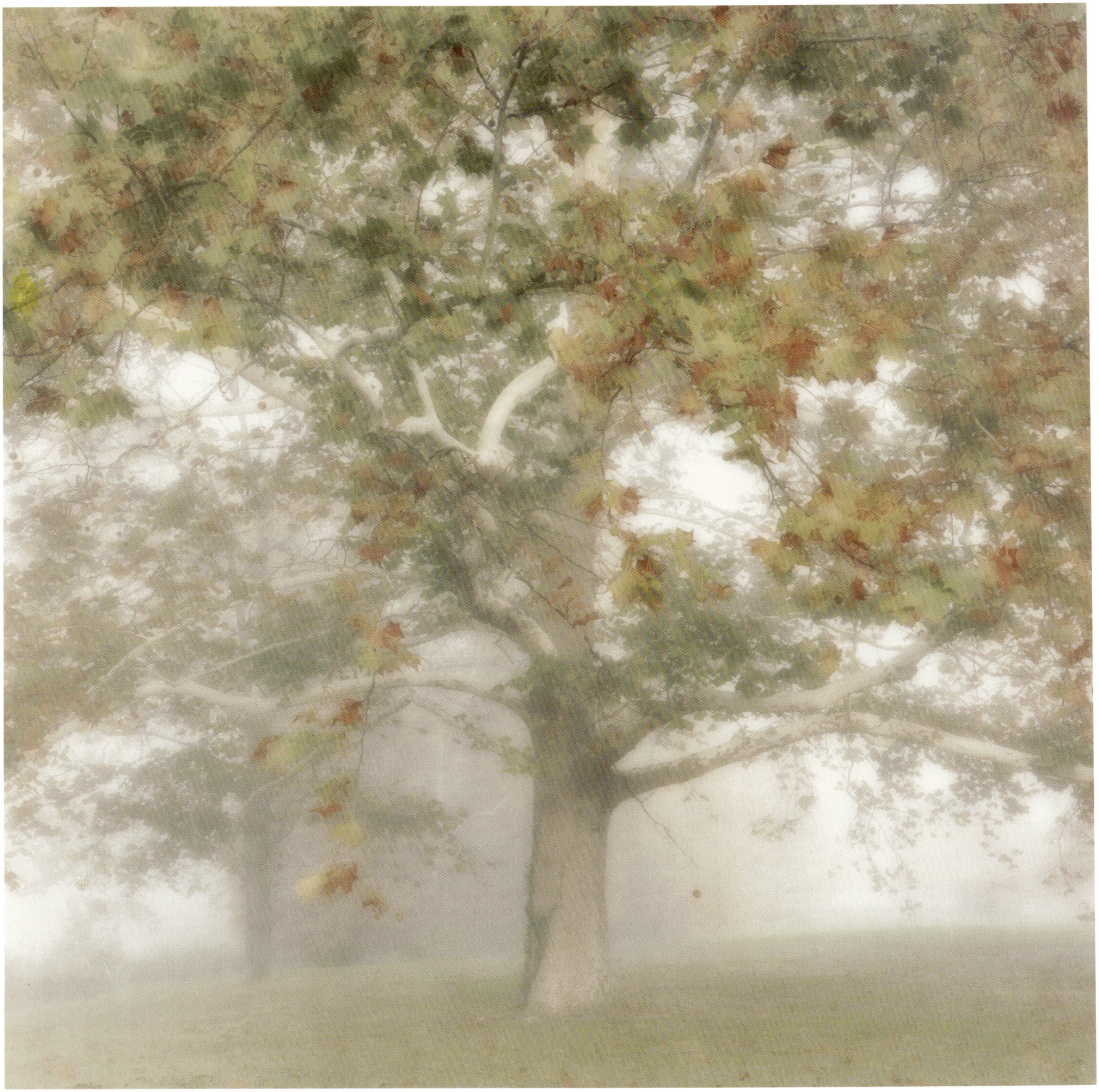

Bernheim Arboretum, Clermont, Kentucky, 1993

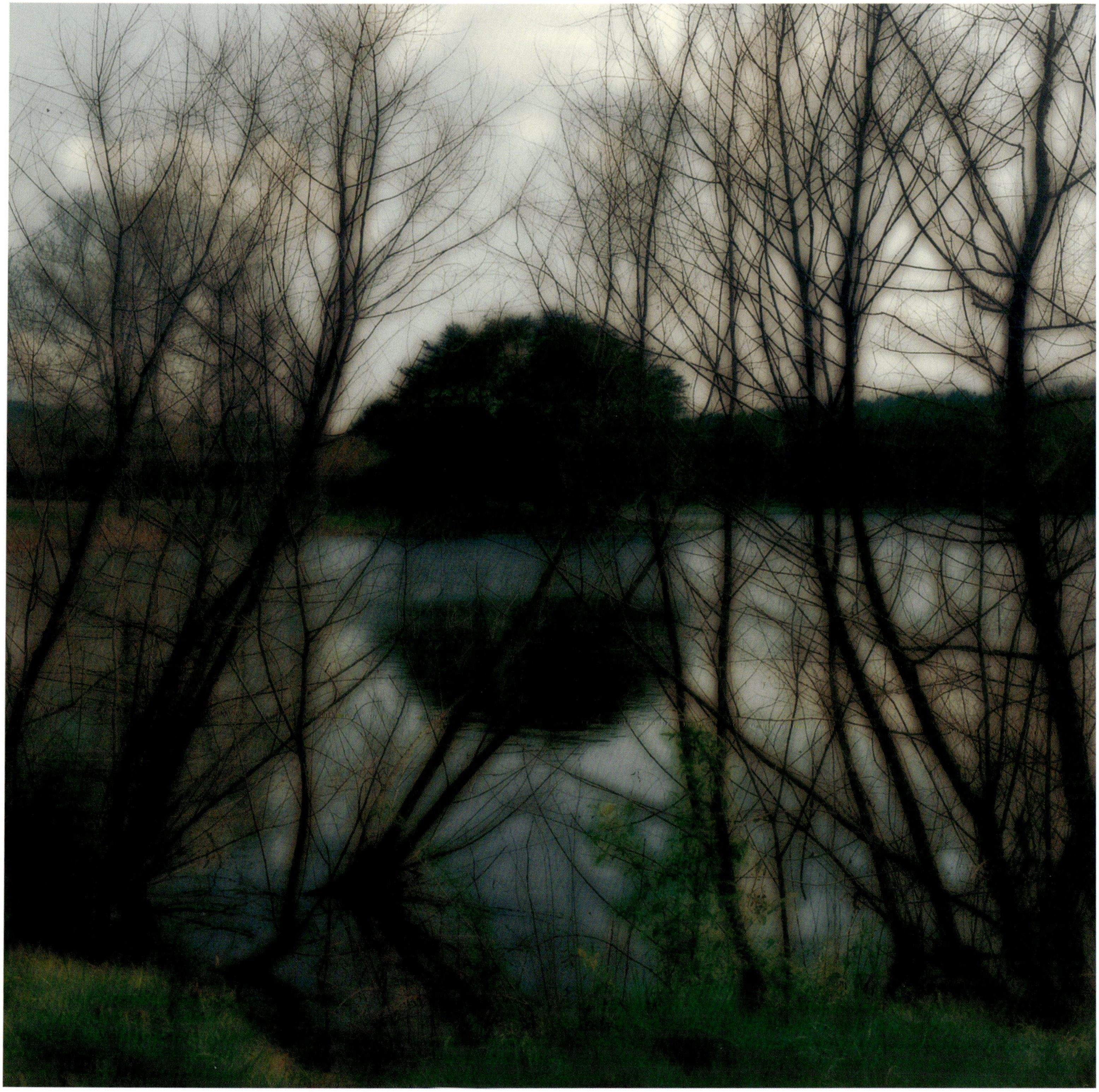

Cheekwood Gardens, Nashville, Tennessee, 2001

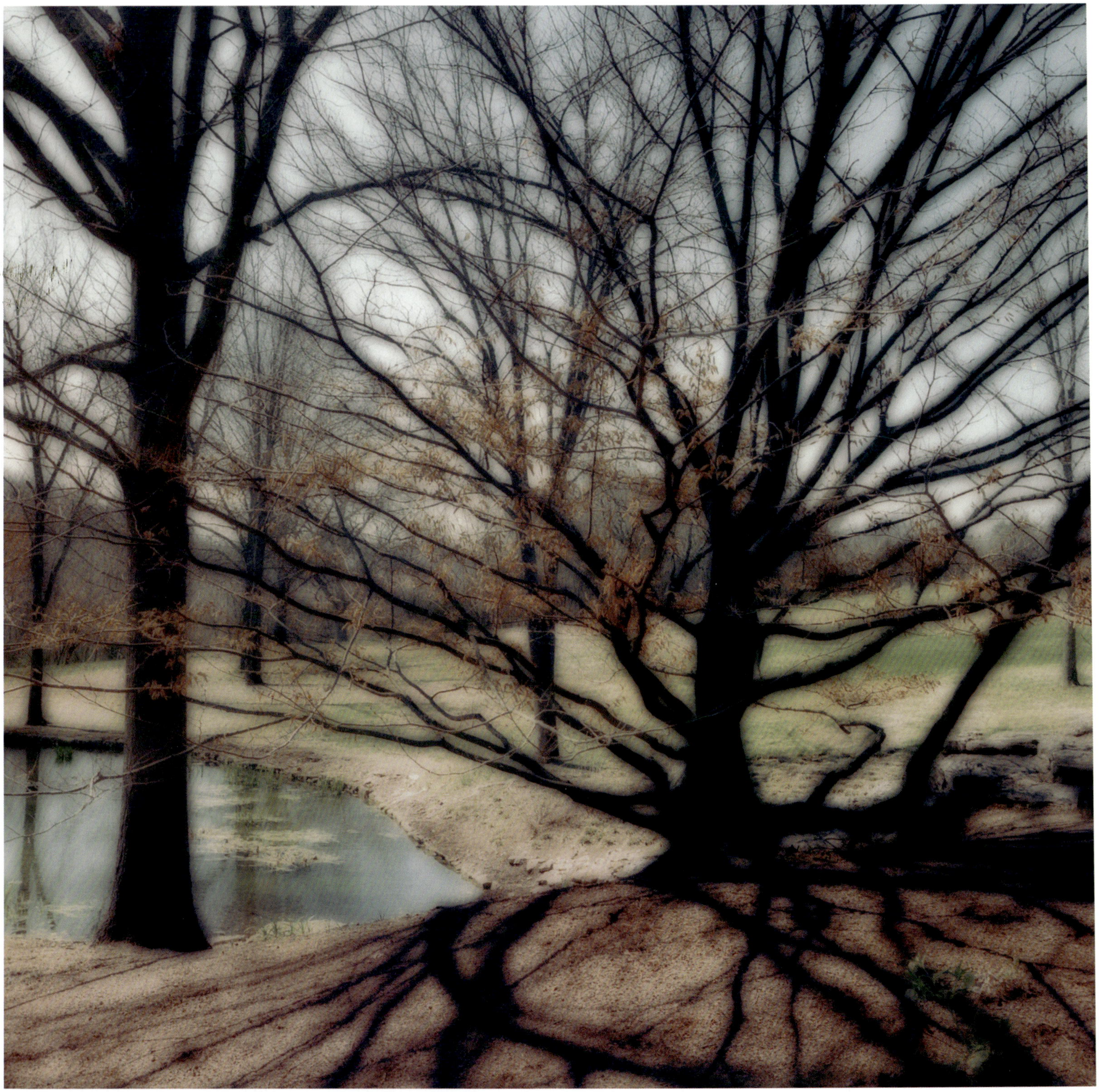

Bernheim Arboretum, Clermont, Kentucky, 1994

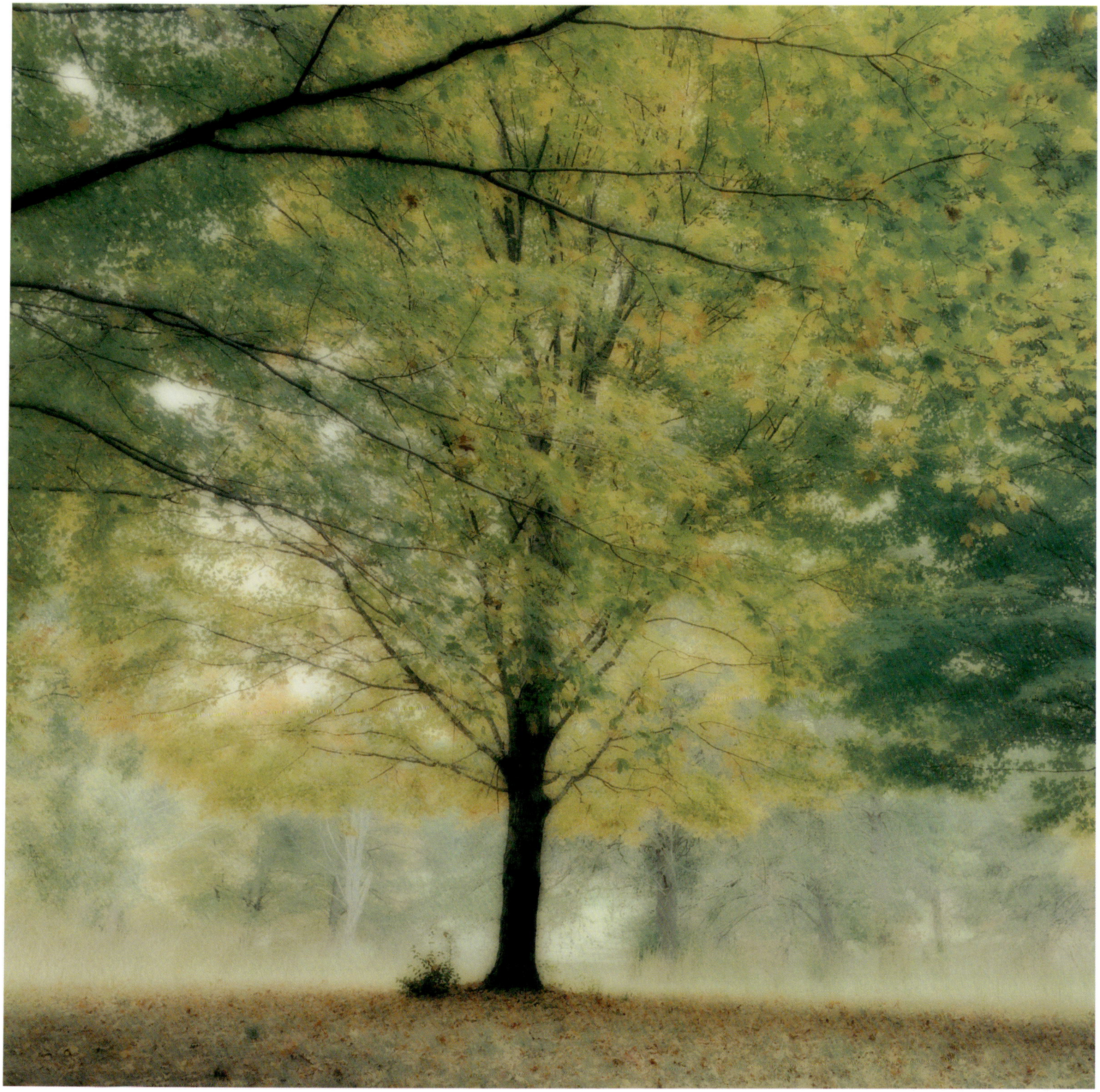

Bernheim Arboretum, Clermont, Kentucky, 1994

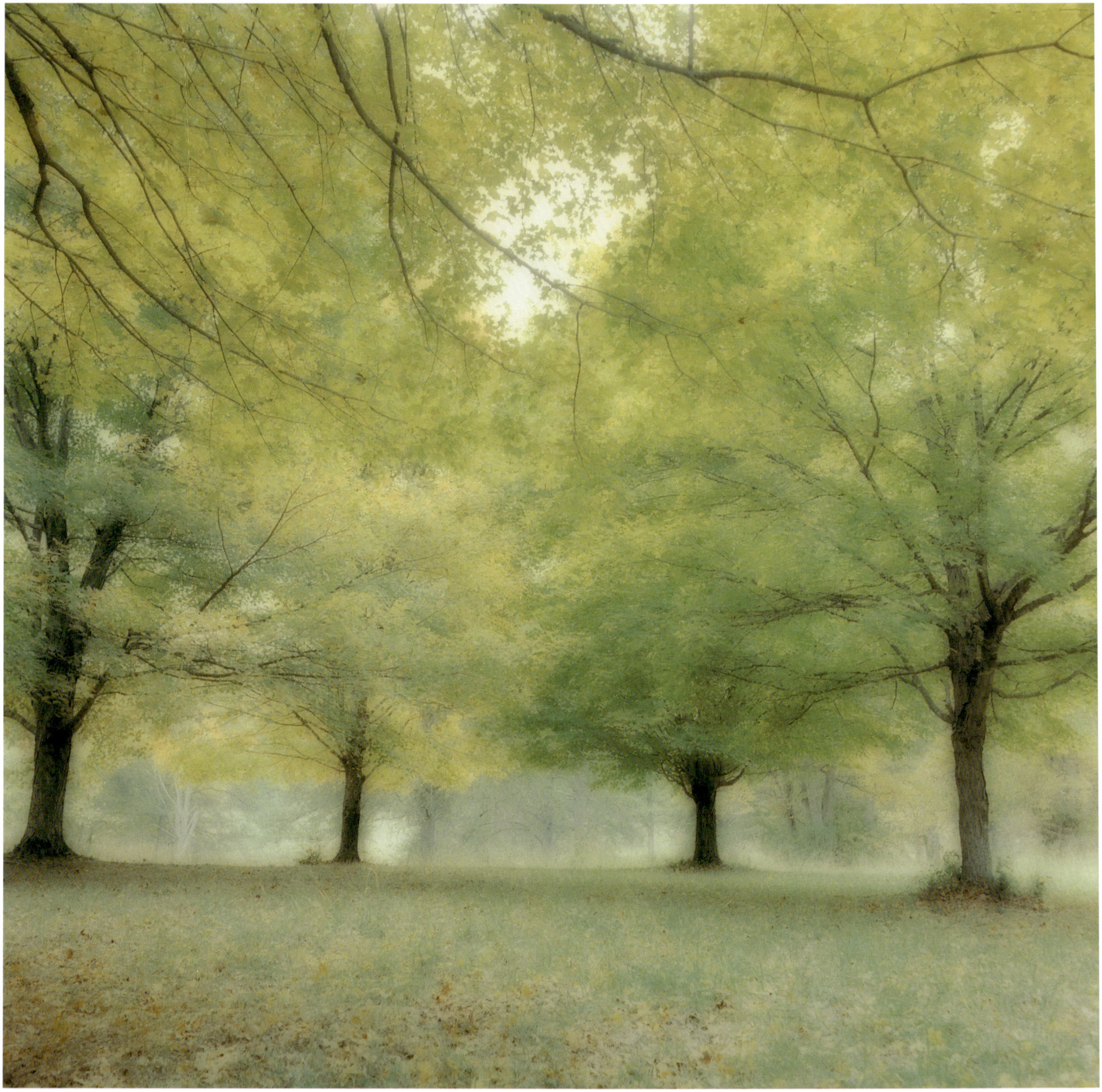

Bernheim Arboretum, Clermont, Kentucky, 2001

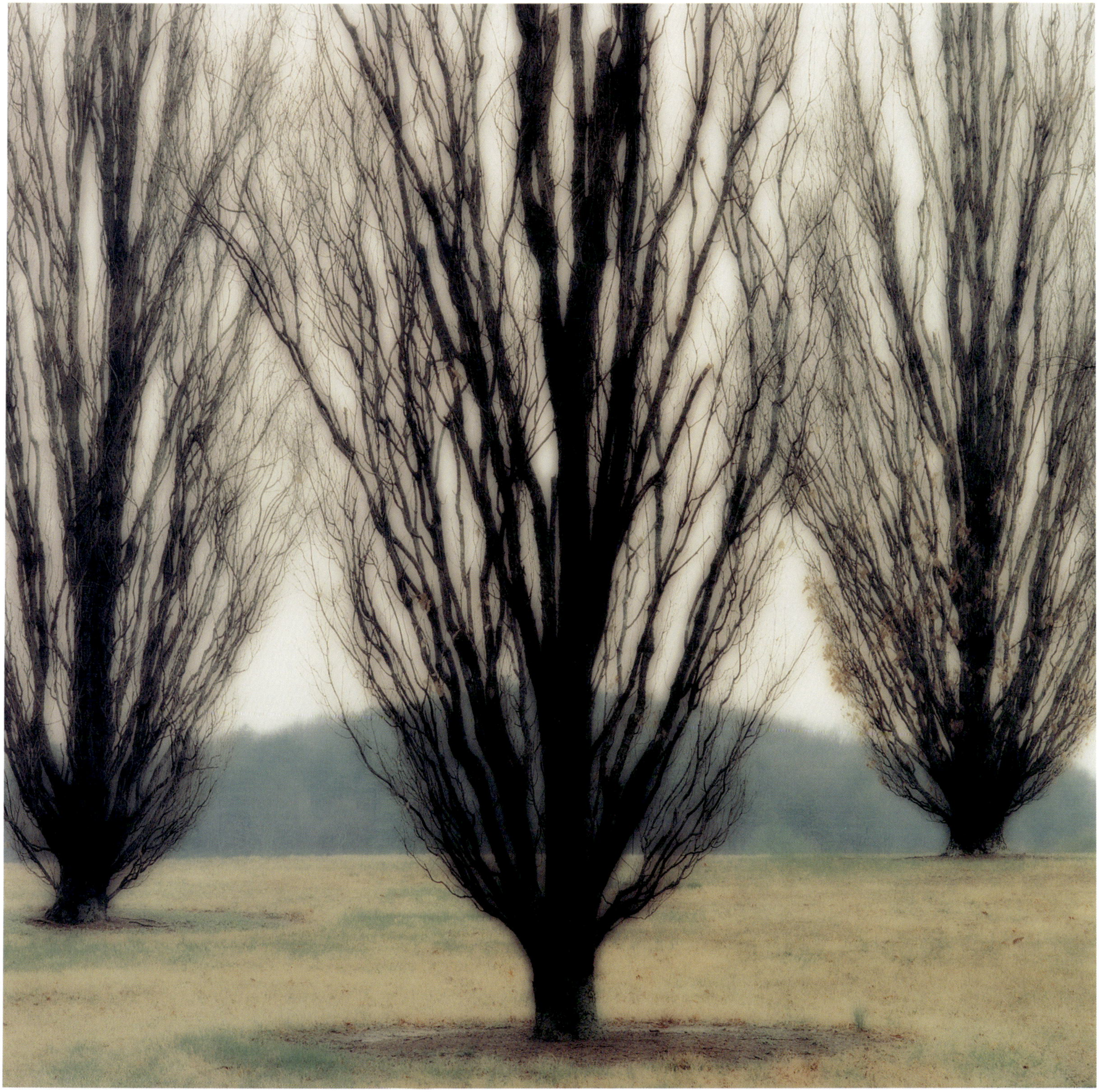

Bernheim Arboretum, Clermont, Kentucky, 1999

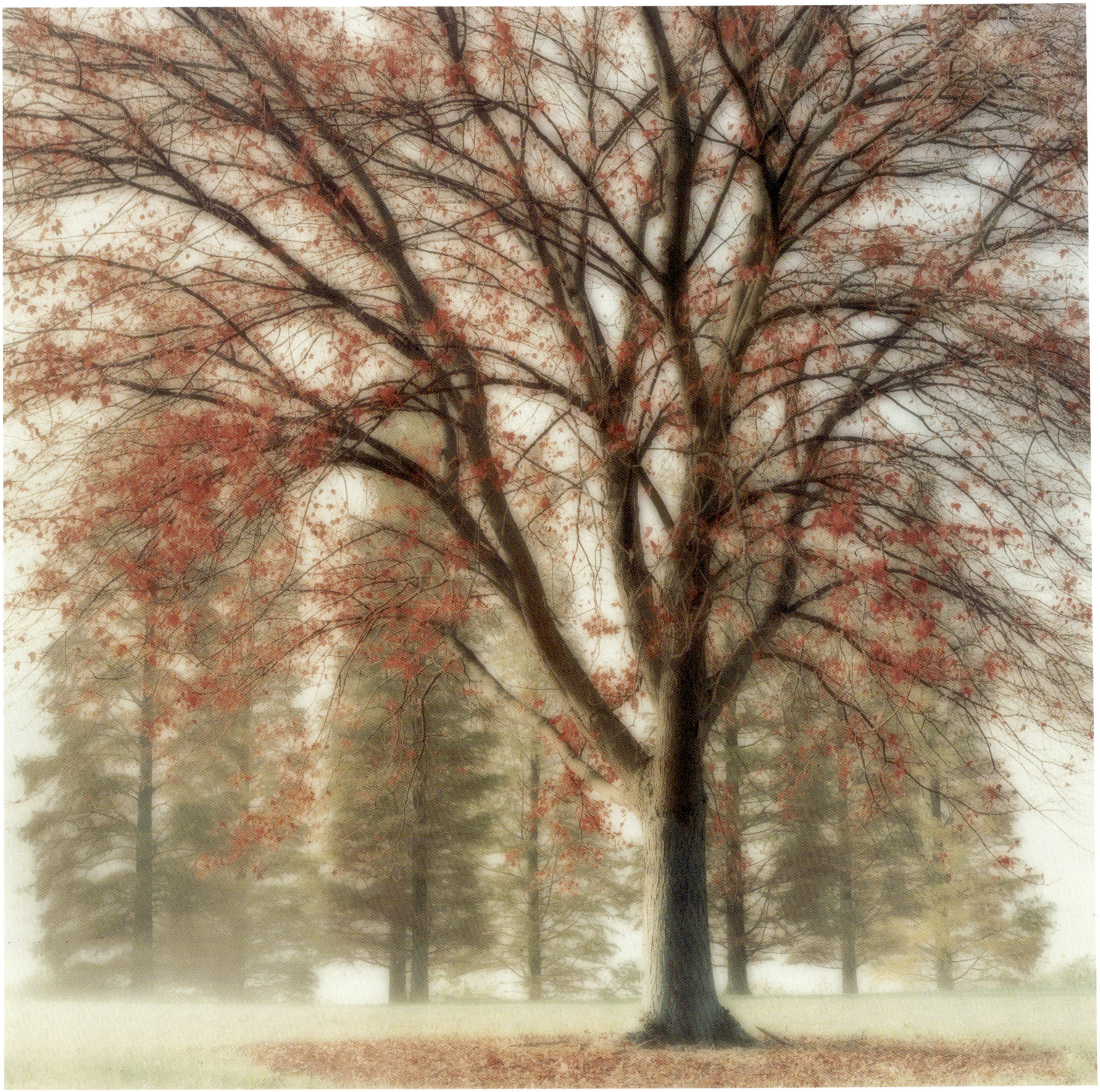

Autumn foliage above a shale bank glows in the morning sun.
The dark rock imposes horizontal structure and the trees a vertical pattern.
This image illustrates the transition from my structured black-and-white to color.

Bernheim Forest, Clermont, Kentucky, 1992

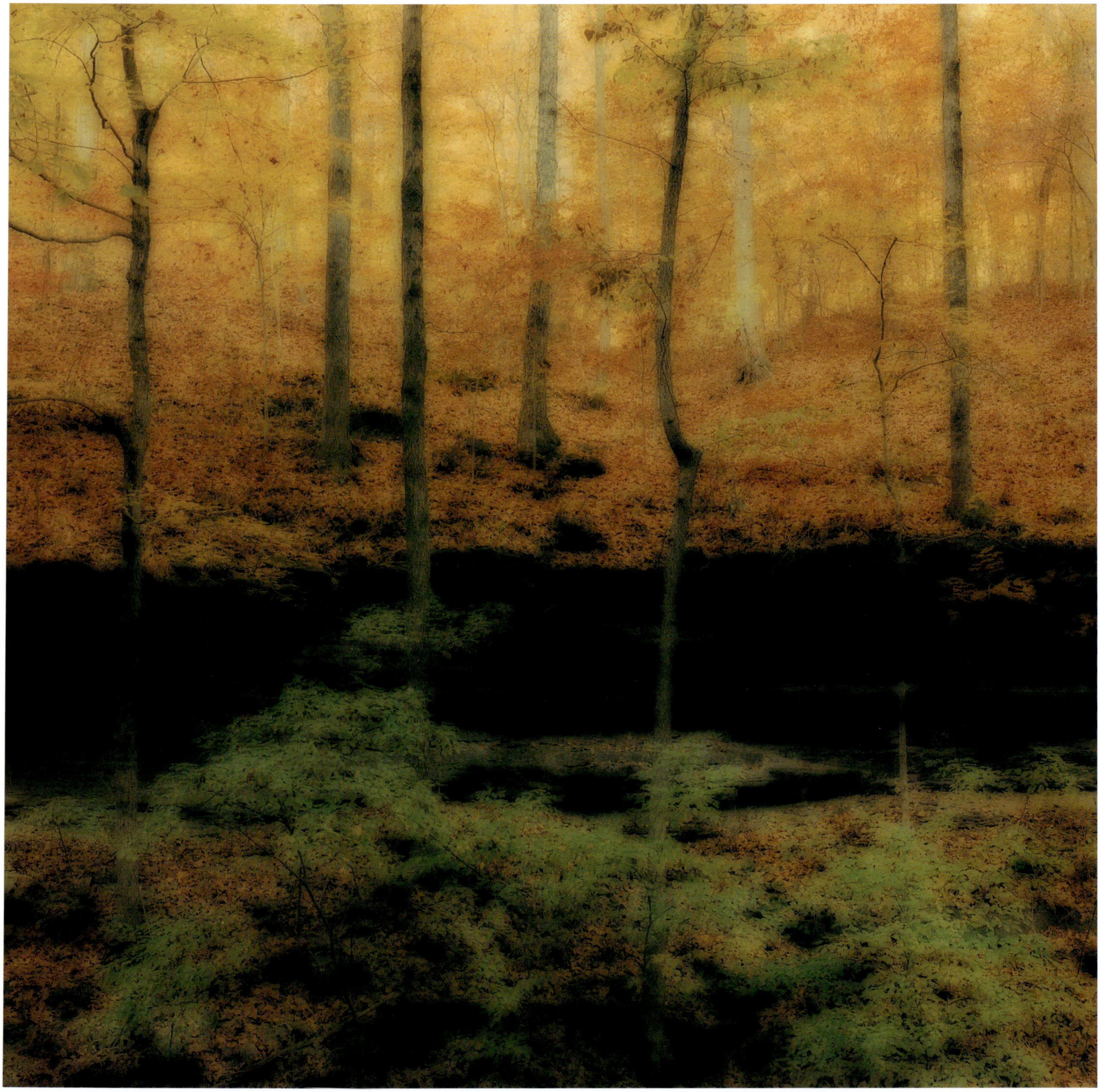

Fort Snelling Park, Minneapolis, Minnesota, 1993

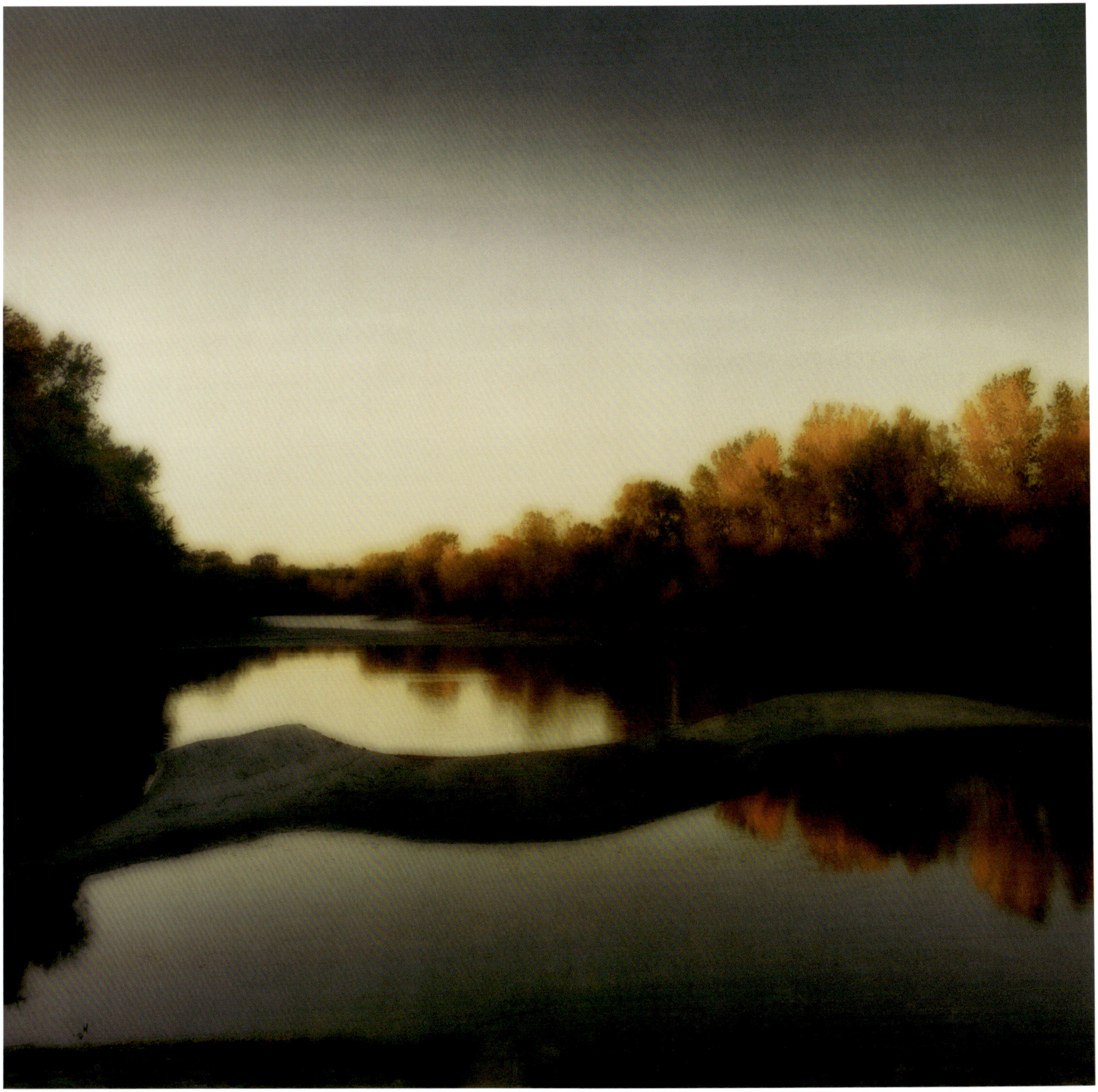

Color film records a monochromatic scheme like this with great subtlety.
I like the brown grass; the air seems as cold as it actually was.

Mendota Bridge, Minneapolis, Minnesota, 1993

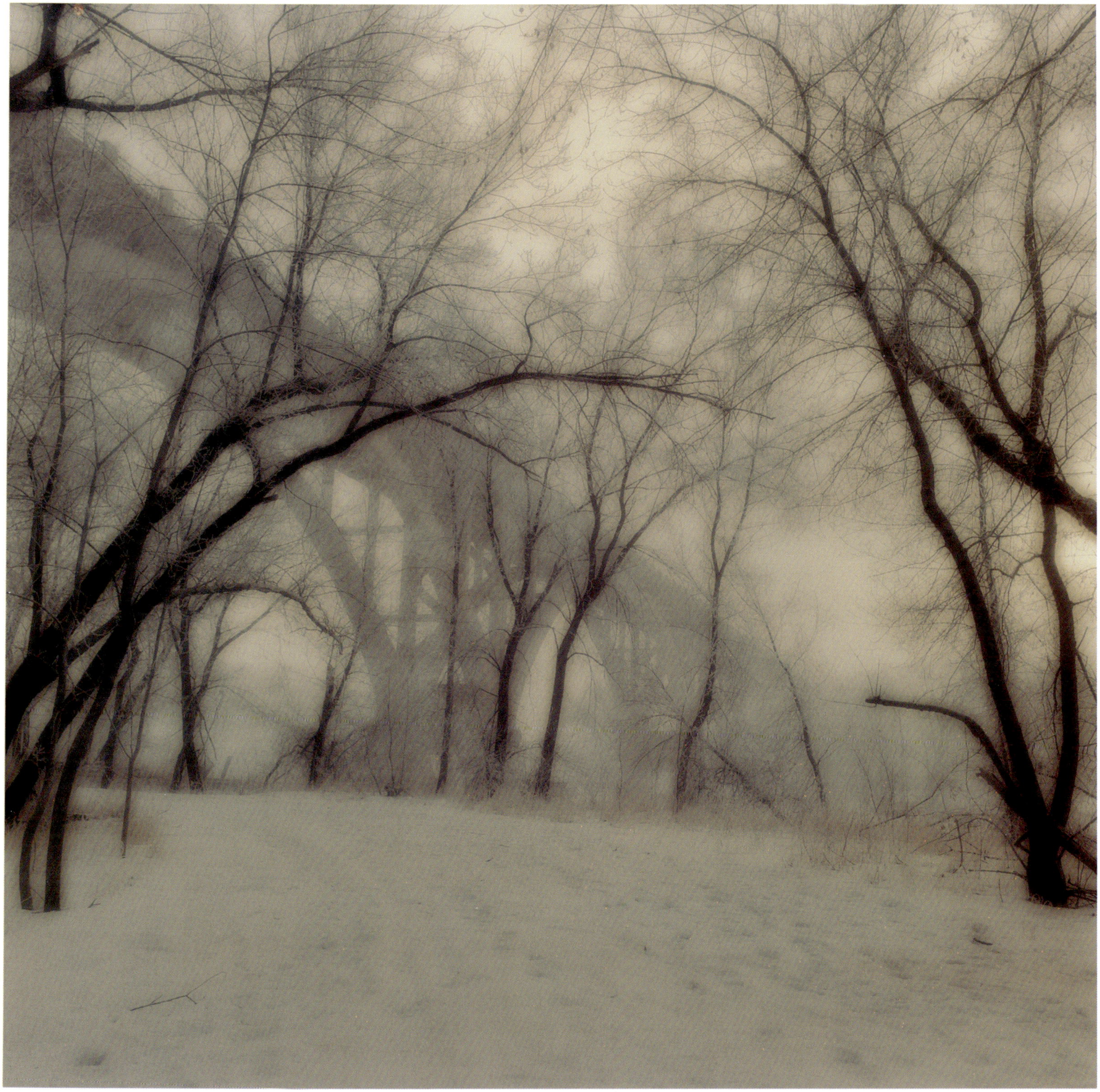

Zemurray Gardens, near Loranger, Louisiana, 2000

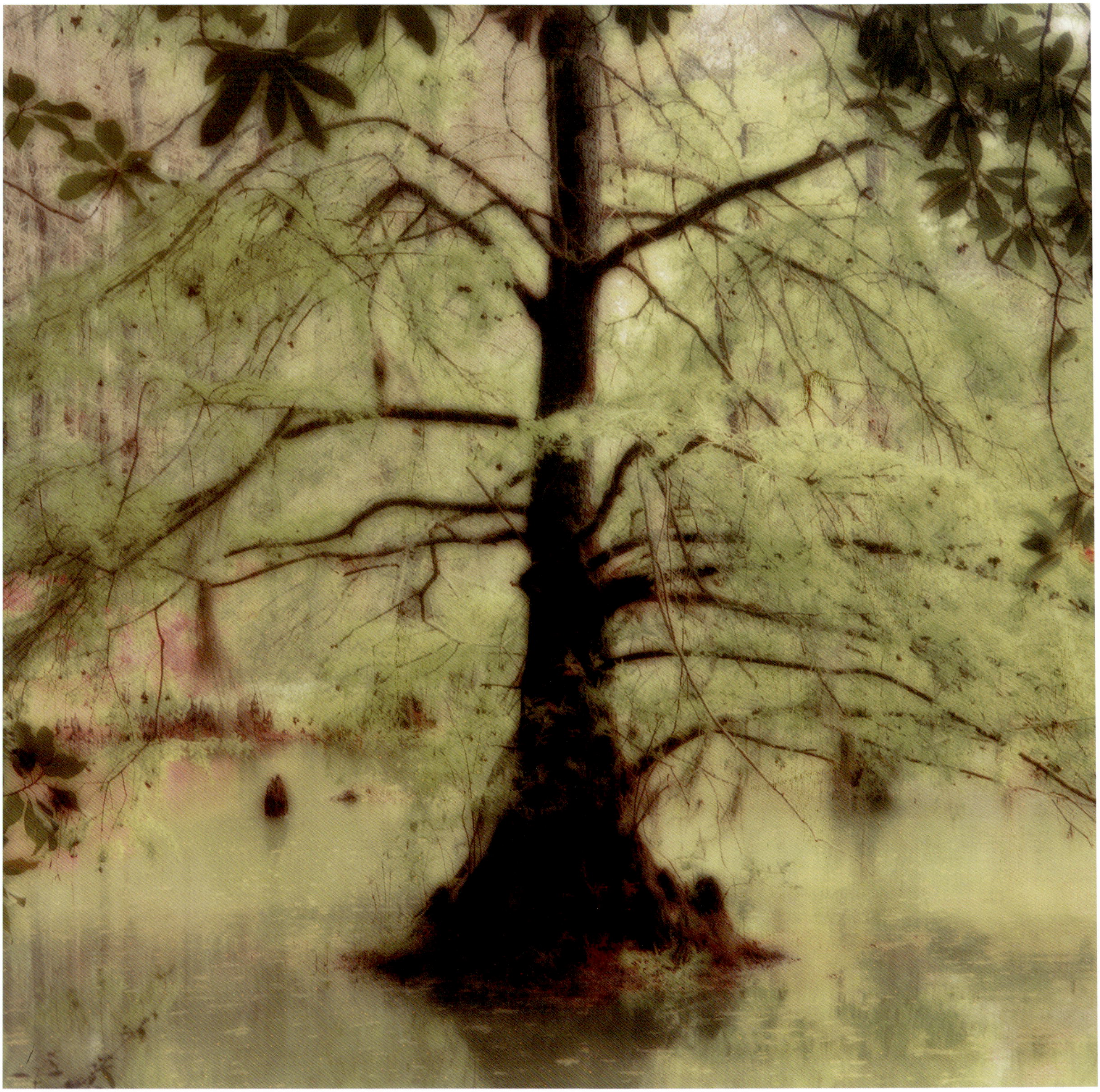

These opalescent colors followed a spring rain.
The green of the lake sets off the pink azaleas.

Zemurray Gardens, near Loranger, Louisiana, 2000

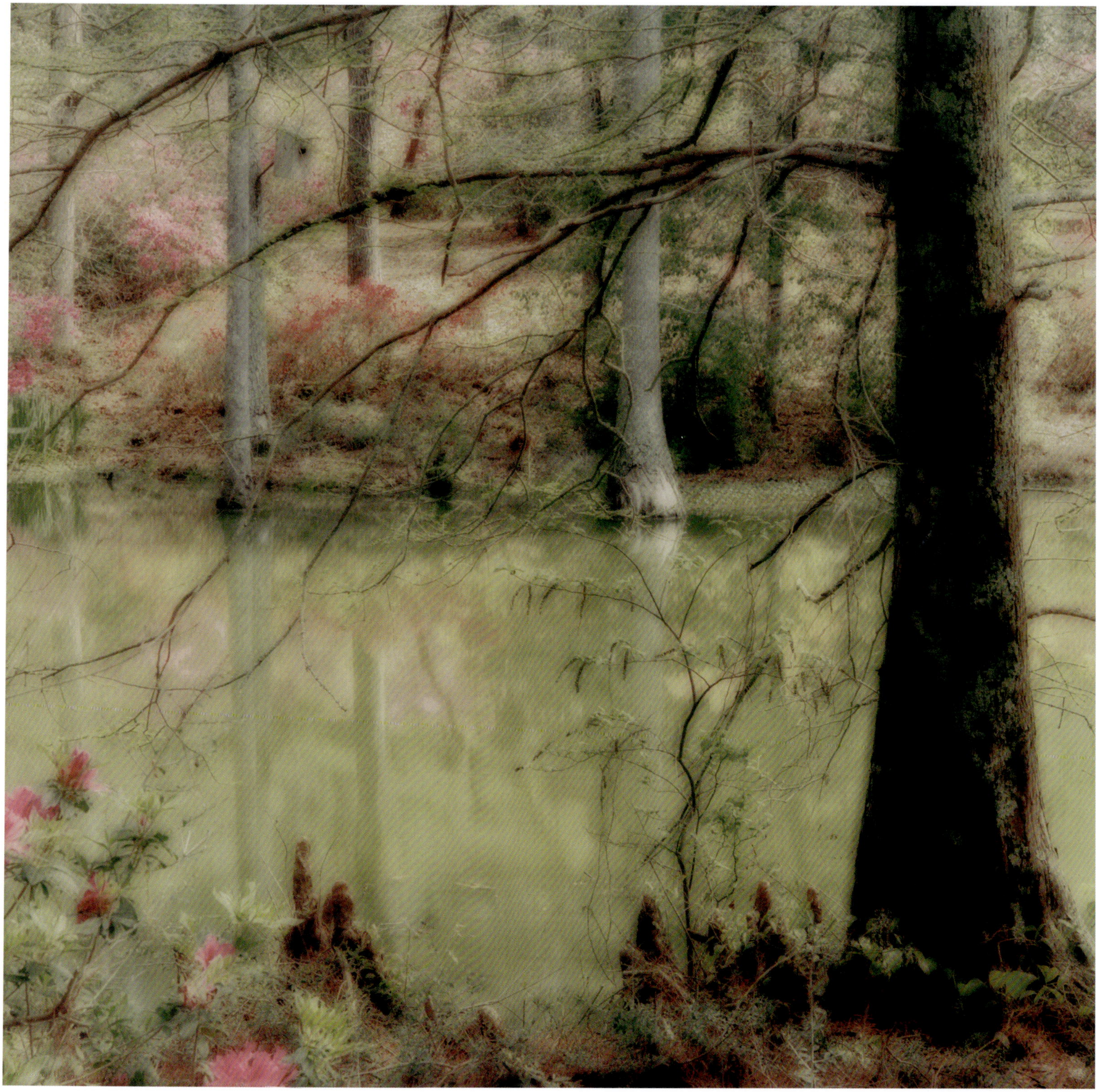

Live Oak Gardens, near New Iberia, Louisiana, 1993

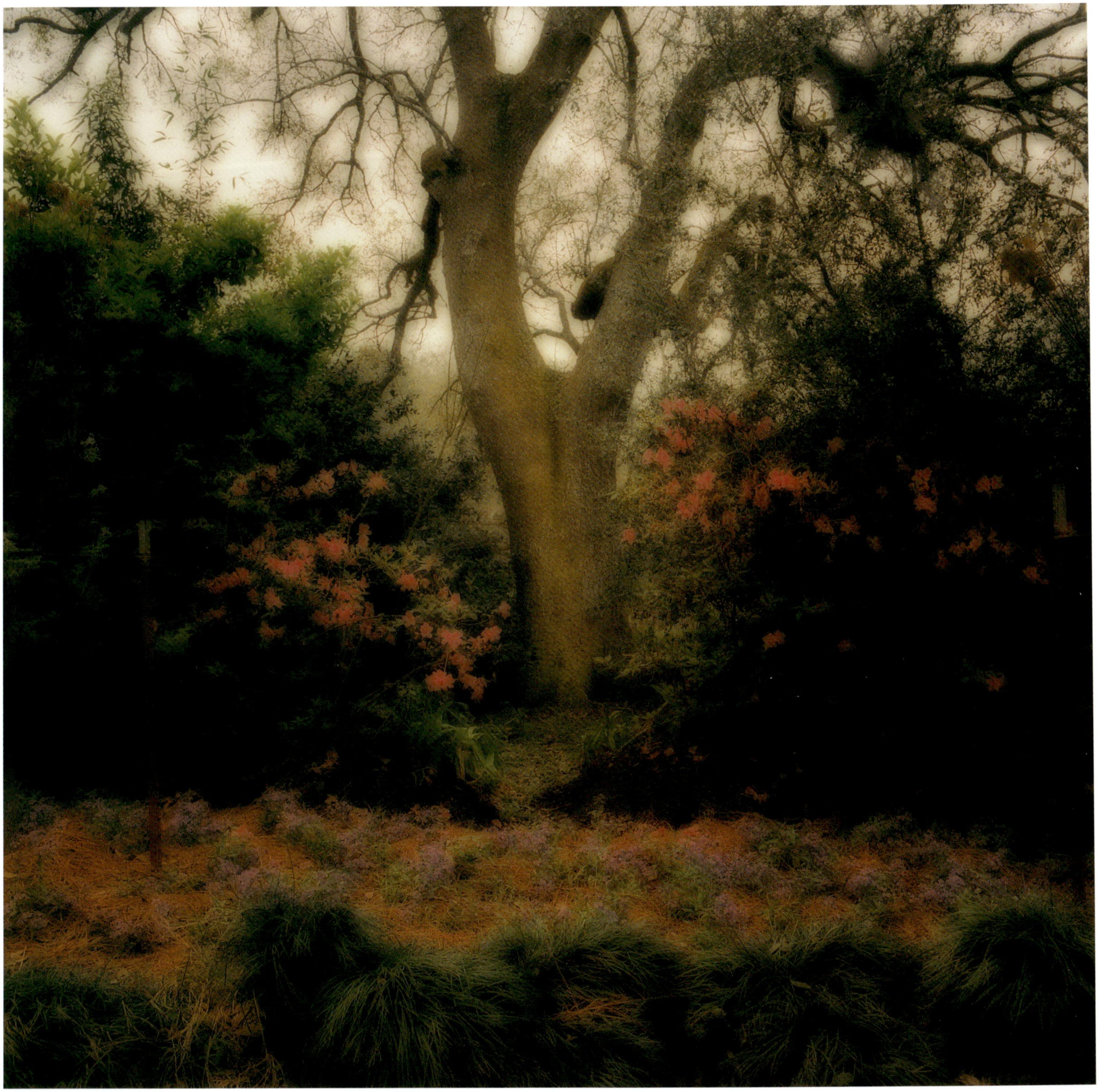

Zemurray Gardens, near Loranger, Louisiana, 2000

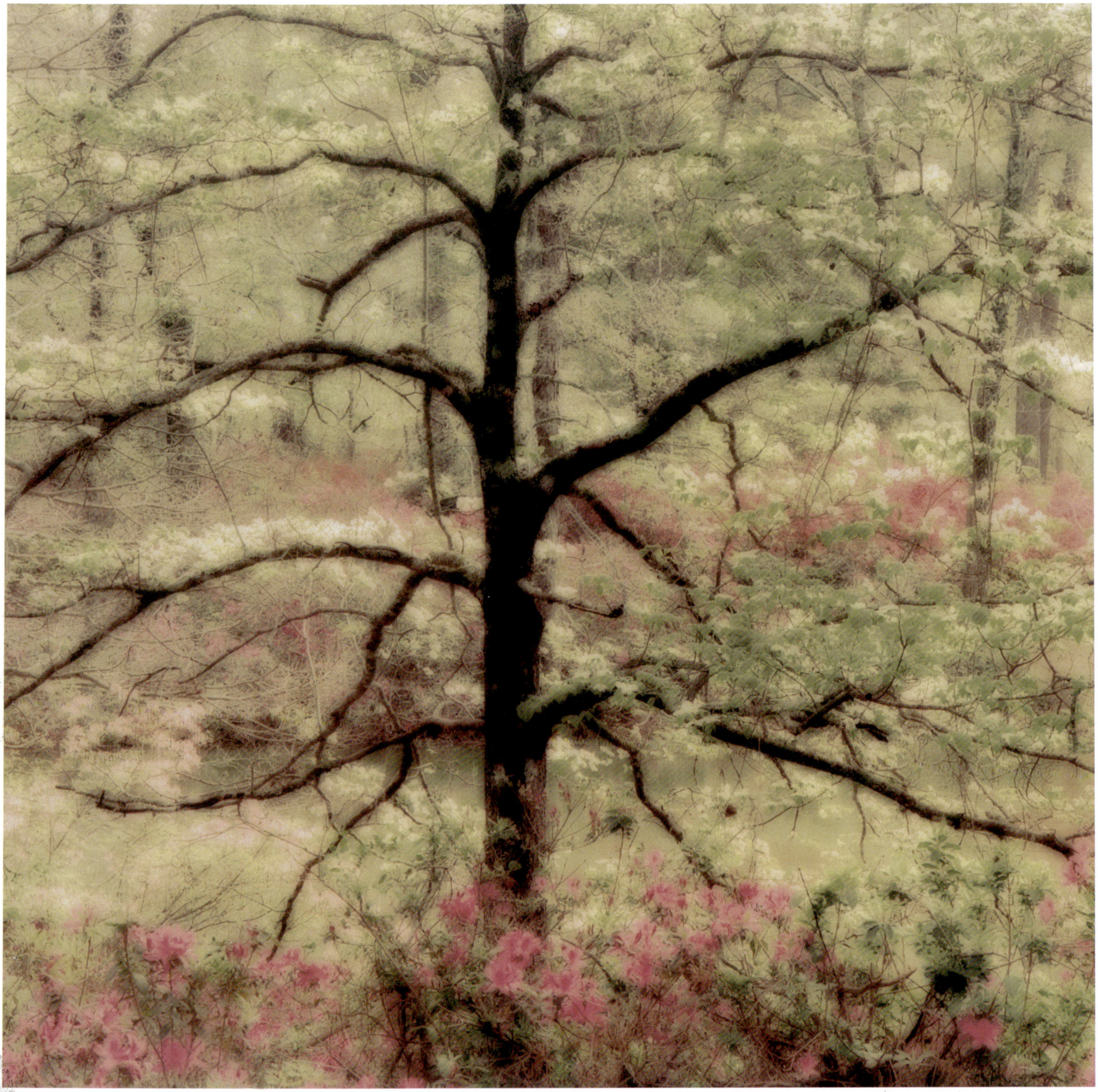

Fallen red camellias define this otherwise monochromatic setting.
Spanish moss hangs from the live oaks — a quintessentially southern scene
near New Iberia, Louisiana, where Edmund McIlhenny first concocted Tabasco sauce.
The factory is still there.

Avery Island, near Lafayette, Louisiana, 1996

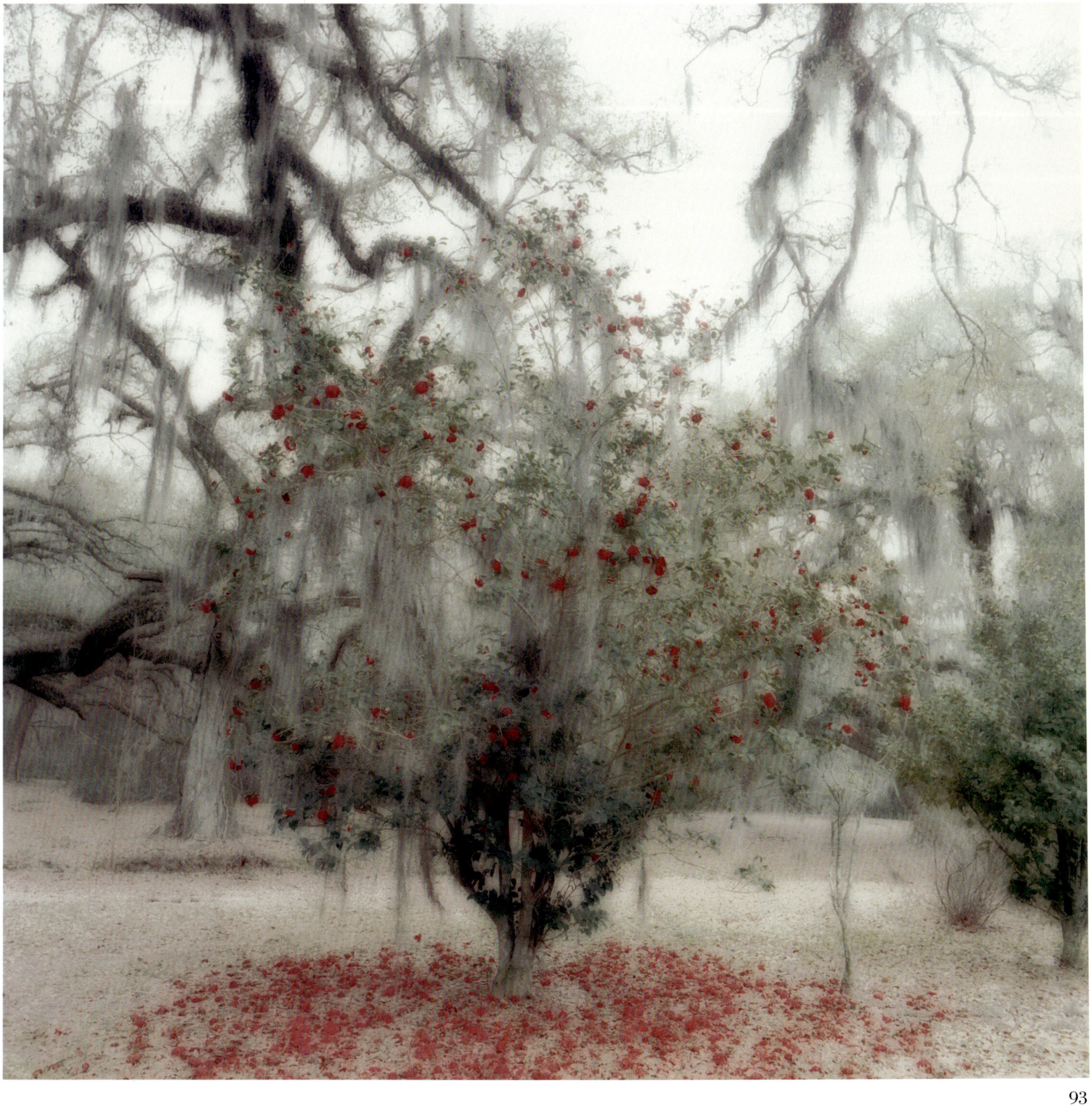

Chiricahua National Monument, near Willcox, Arizona, 1994

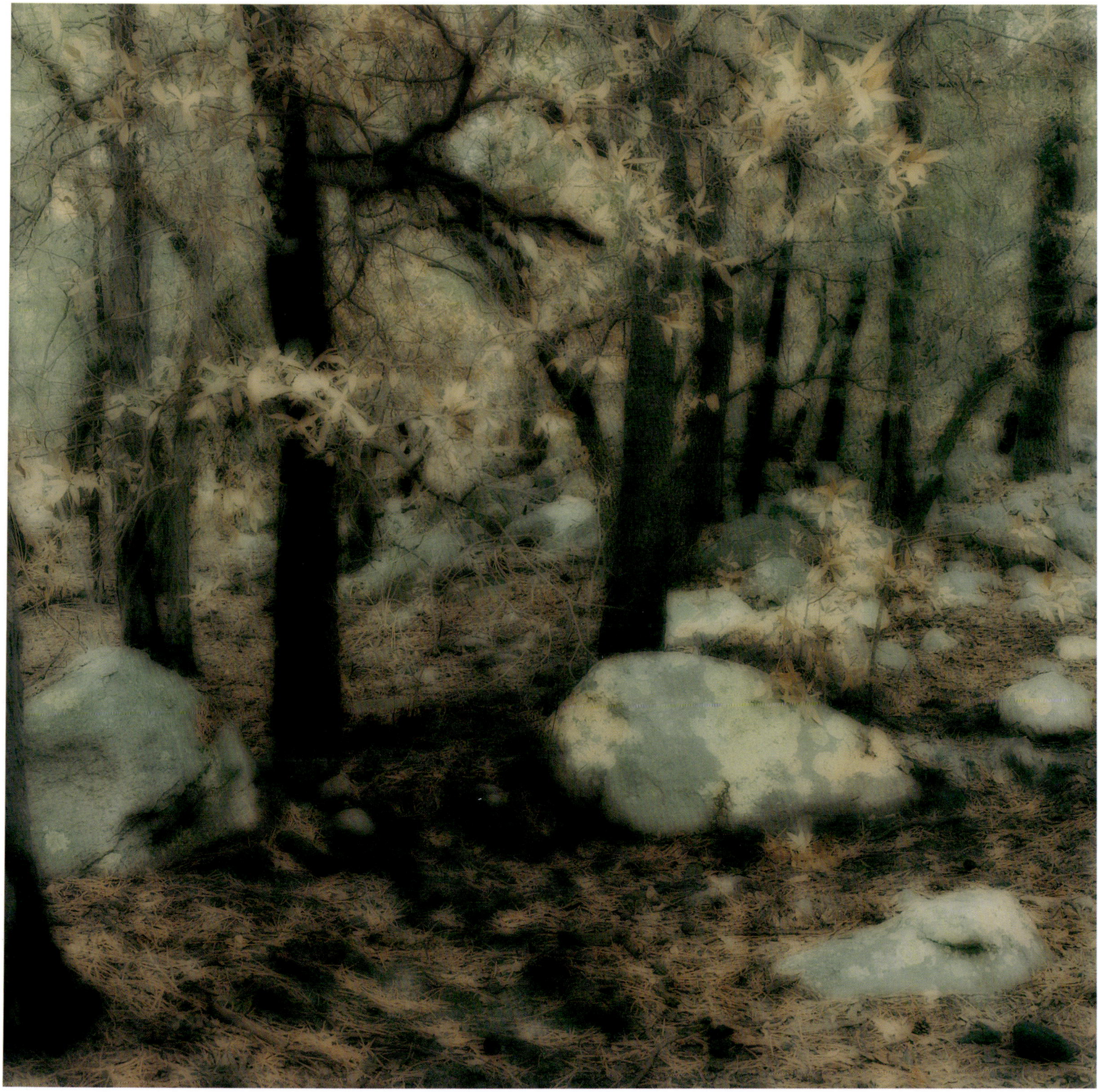

An empty stage, set with luminescent algae-covered rocks:
this is an early venture into texture, shape, and color.

Chiricahua National Monument, near Willcox, Arizona, 1994

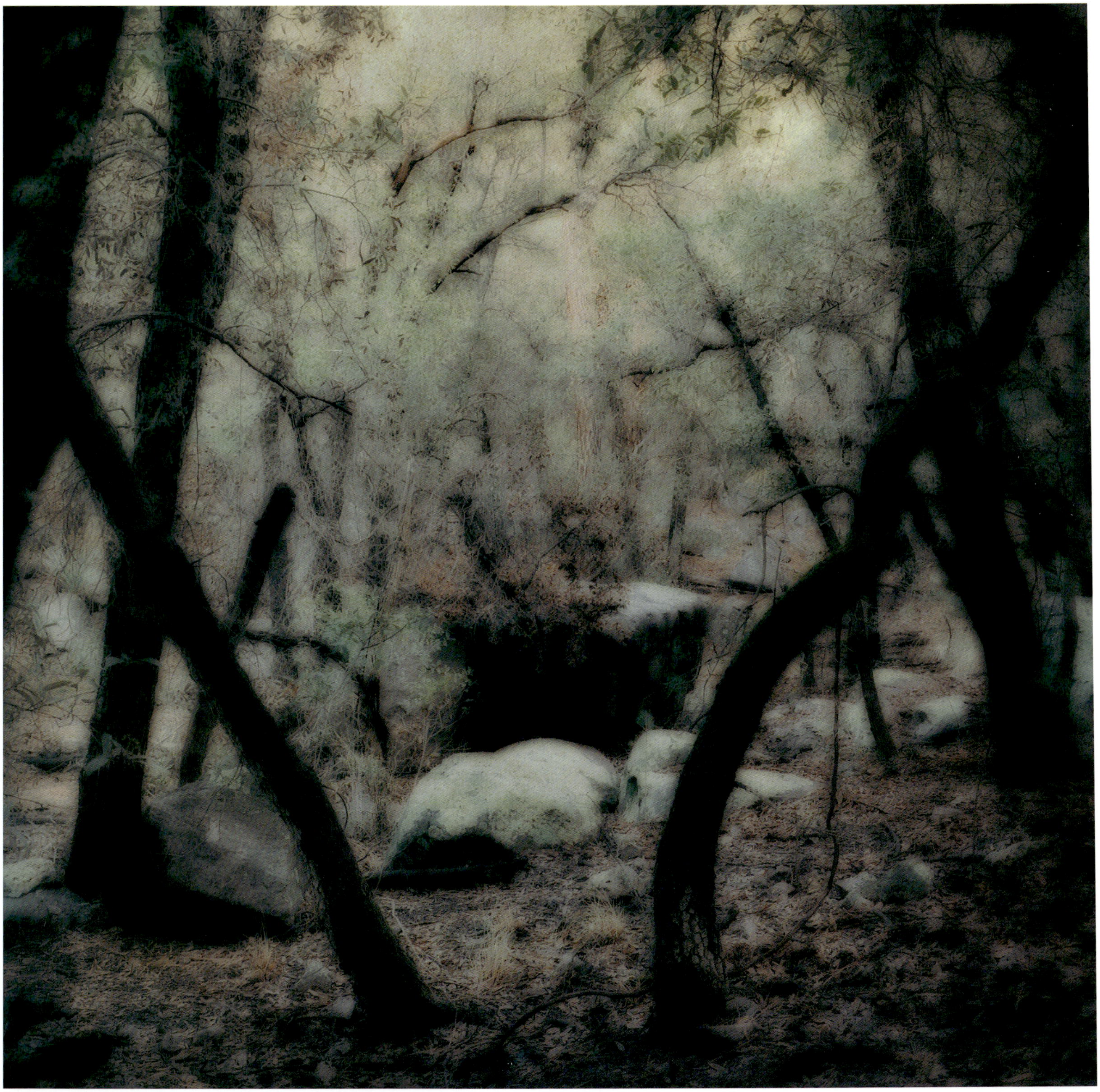

It's not difficult to fill the viewfinder with flowers on a perfect spring day at Filoli. The pure density was amazing; I can't remember how I ever found room to stand with the tulips pushing out toward me.

Filoli Gardens, Woodside, California, 2000

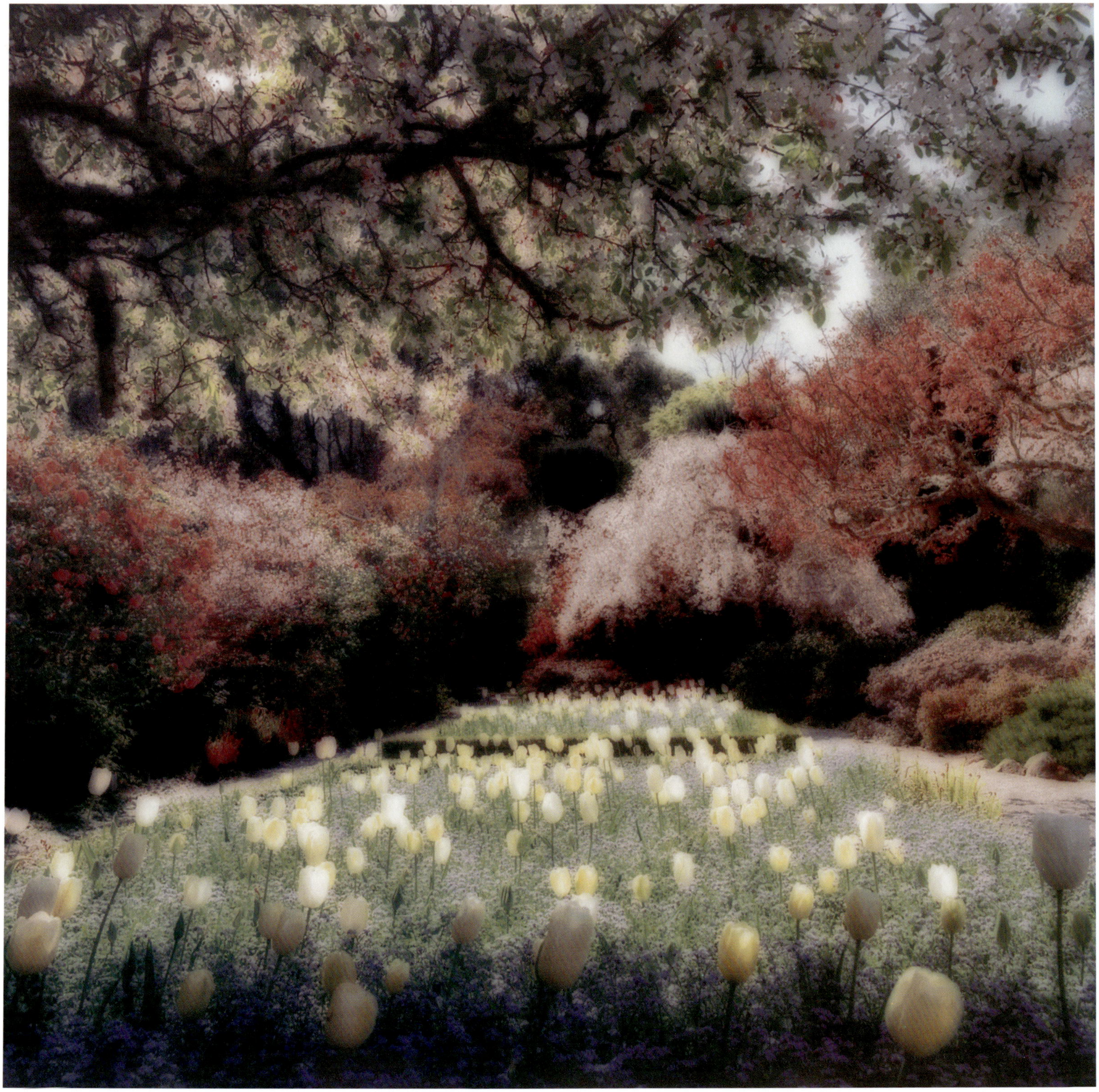

Filoli Gardens, Woodside, California, 2000

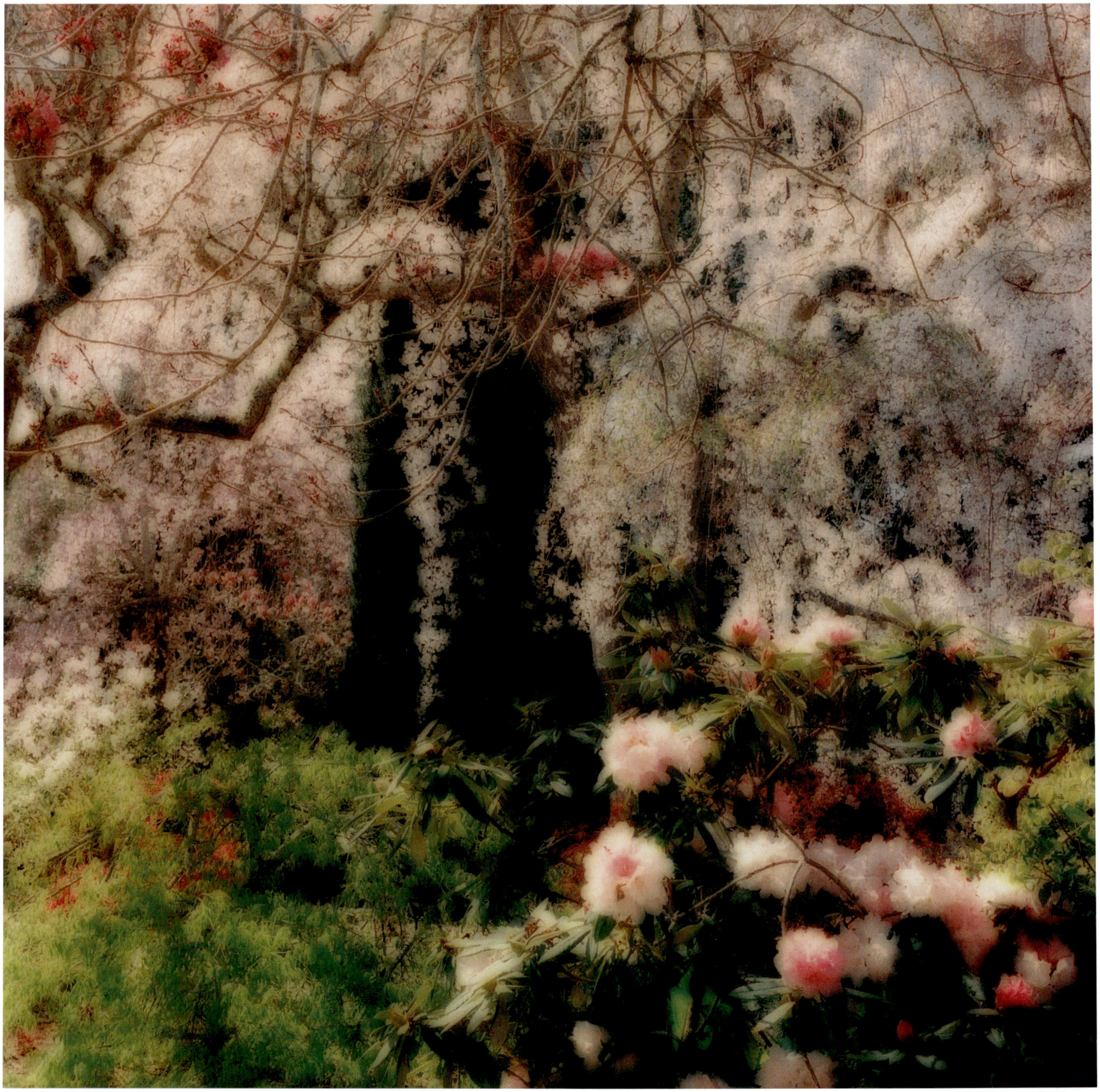

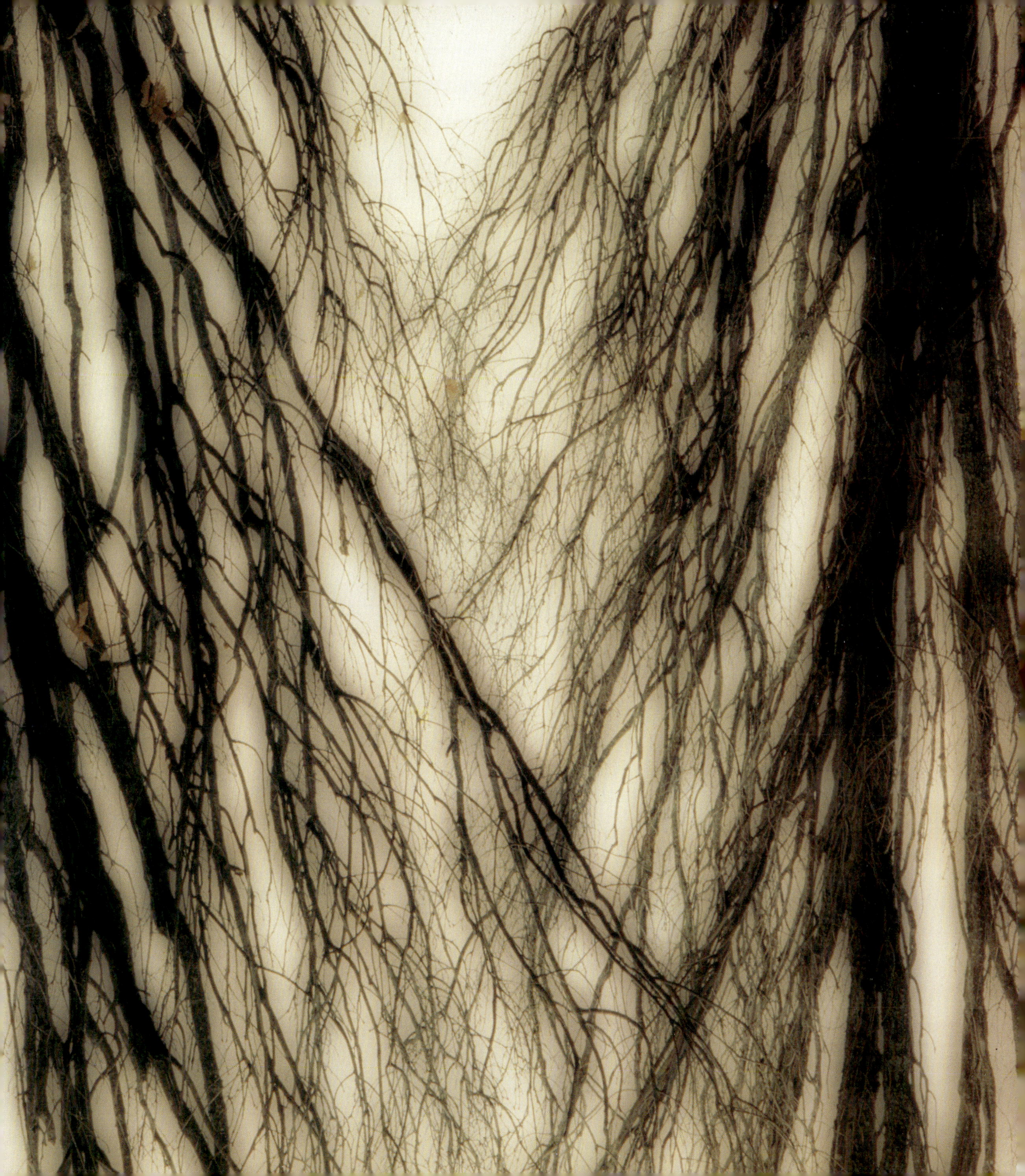

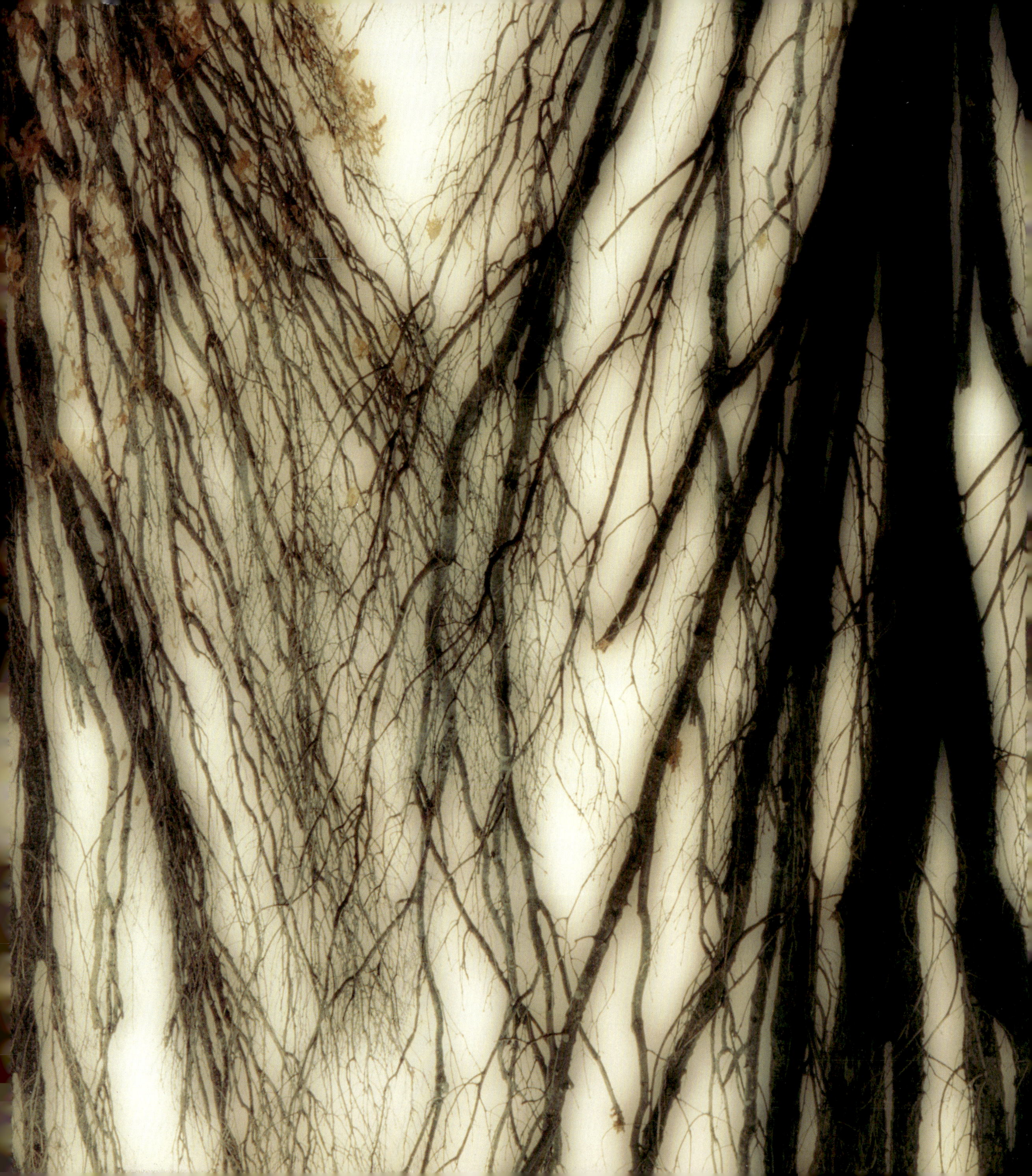

Near Tulum, Mexico, 2002

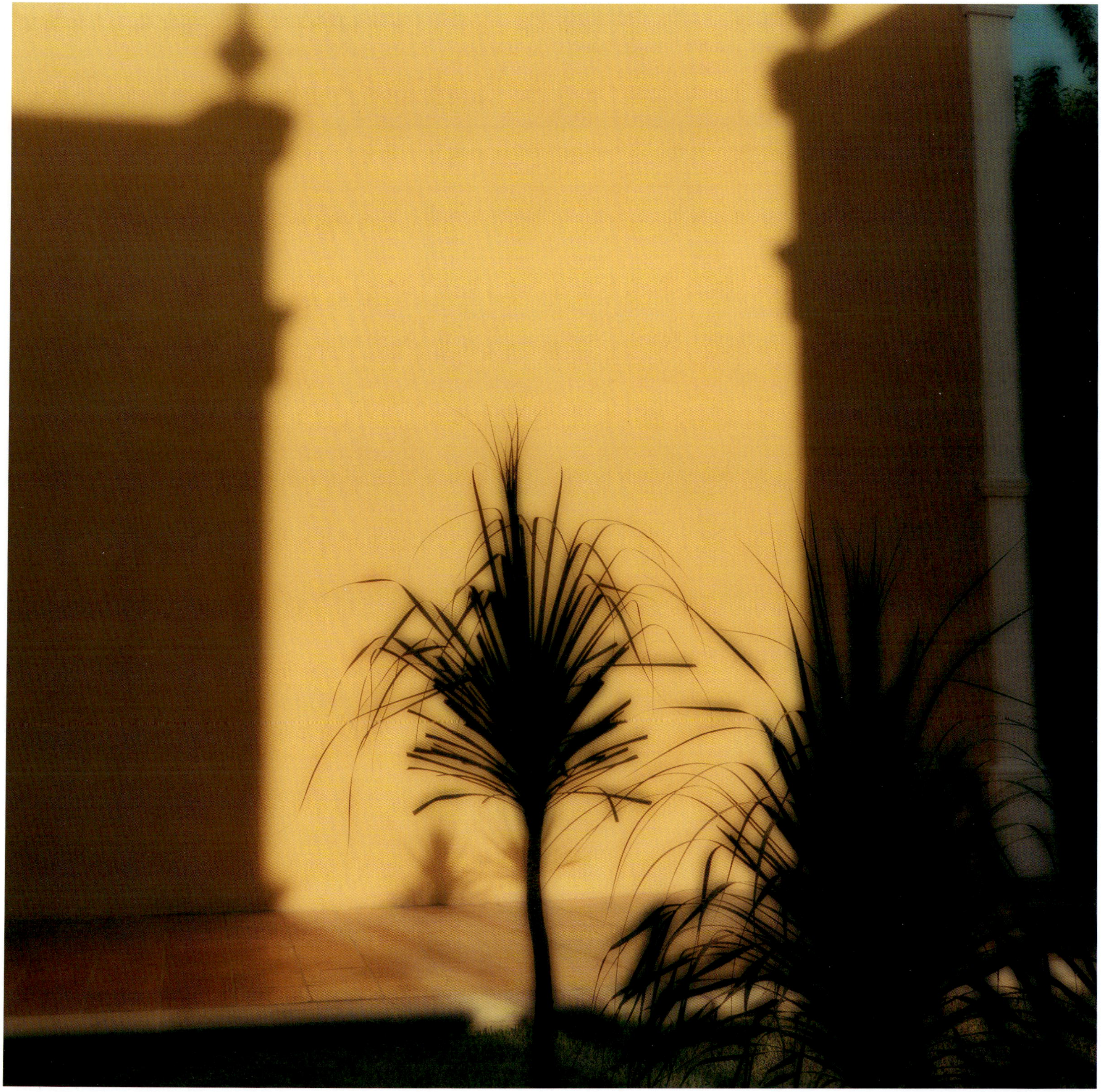

This photograph is about the color and light of Mexico
and the design of palms and shadows.

Near Tulum, Mexico, 2002

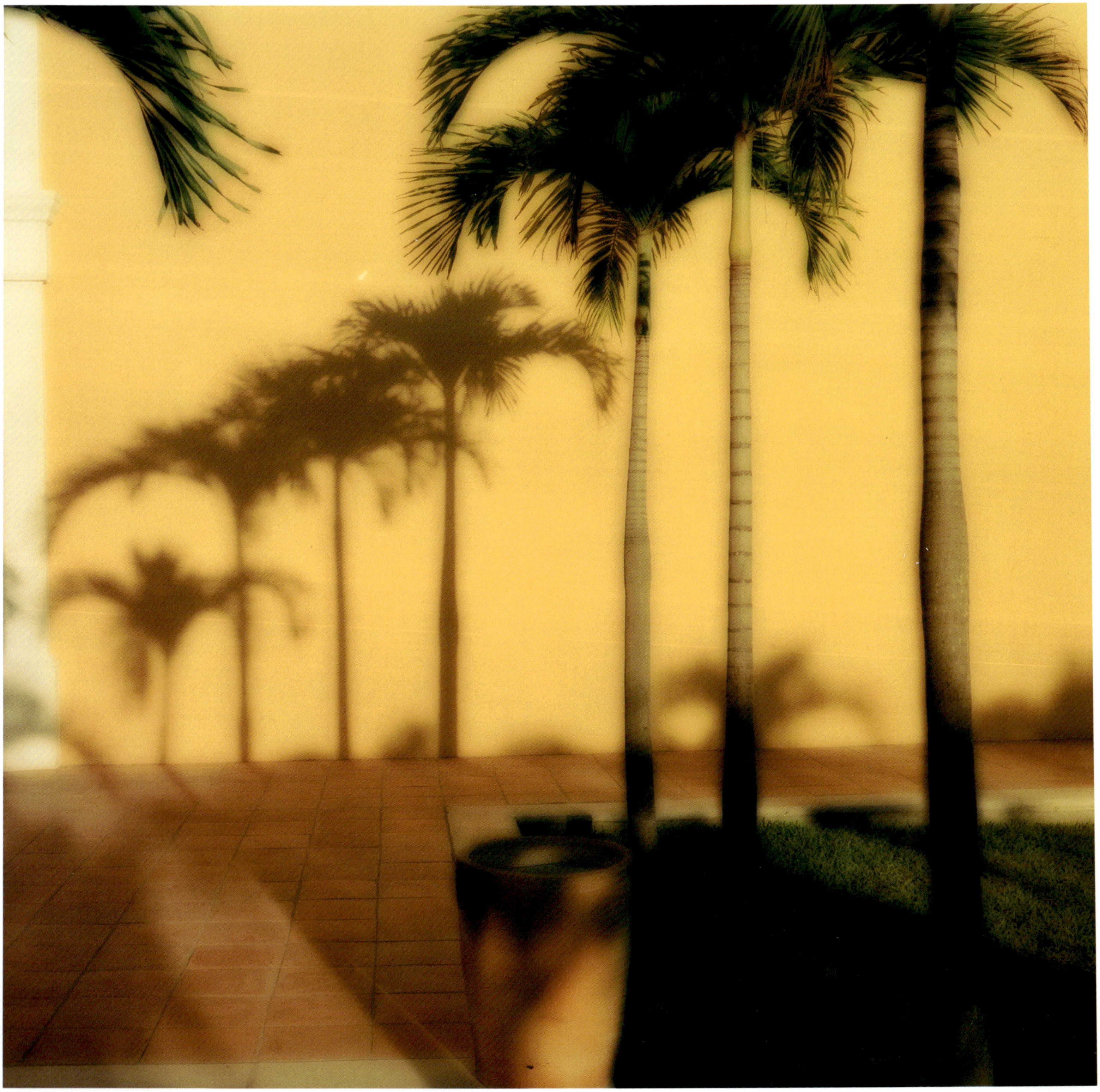

Near Tulum, Mexico, 2002

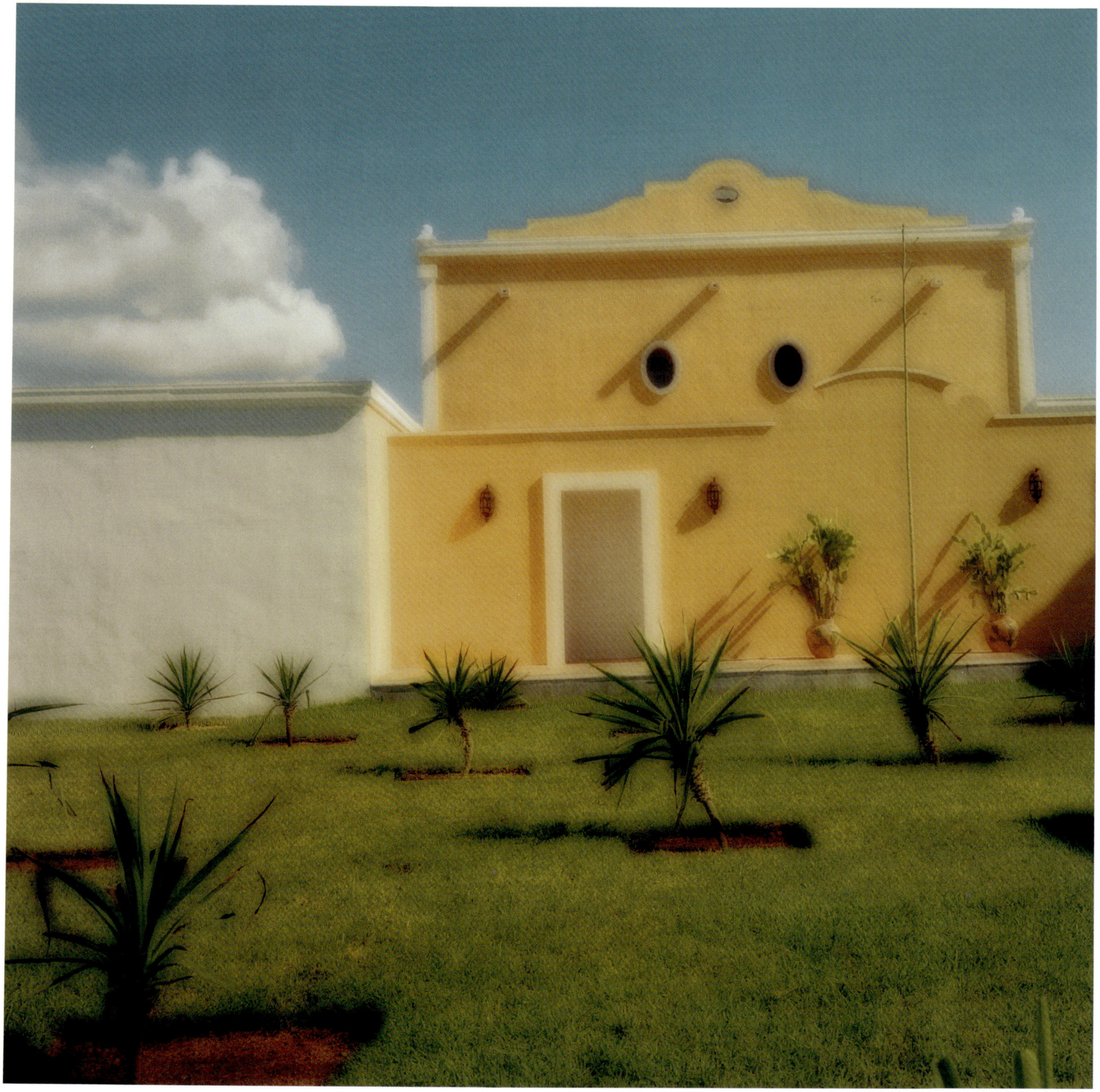

INTERVIEW WITH LYNN GEESAMAN

by Verlyn Klinkenborg

KLINKENBORG: I'm curious about what draws you into a landscape when you're out scouting. How do you first approach these scenes? What do you really see through the mind's eye of the lens?

GEESAMAN: First of all, the camera that I use is one that has a waist-level, ground-glass-screen viewfinder. I look down at it and I see the image reversed. I see the image abstracted from what's really out there in front of me.

And that's how I find the landscape. I put myself in a favorable place where I expect to find structure, geometry, and formality. And then I find the image strictly by walking around looking down.

So what I'm seeing is little images that have nothing much to do with awareness of the place.

It's just like I'm finding them by surprise. I've disassociated myself from where I am.

KLINKENBORG: So the camera is a tool that abstracts your subject for you.

GEESAMAN: That's right. If I try to use a conventional camera where I look straight forward through the viewfinder — and if I can actually walk along and not trip when I use a camera like that — I can't function as well because I've lost my sense of disengagement.

KLINKENBORG: I'd never really thought of the viewfinder as a moving tool, the way you describe it.

GEESAMAN: It is. I'm looking down all the time. That's why one of my big fears is working on uneven ground.

KLINKENBORG: Yes, I can imagine.

GEESAMAN: The feelings that I have when I go to these places are not ones of great awe and inspiration and happiness. Usually I feel insecure and threatened. And as my husband said — and this is true — we feel like a couple of fugitives often, as though somebody's going to come up to us and say, "Where's your permit to do this?" And this has happened.

So there's a lot of insecurities and worries associated with this whole job of taking the picture, let alone whether the equipment's going to fail and I'm going to be cold. I'm always cold and wet. It seems that we're there only in the off-season.

KLINKENBORG: But absolutely none of that translates in the photographs at all.

GEESAMAN: No, it doesn't. It's a restoration of something that wasn't a glorious experience at all.

KLINKENBORG: And yet the photographs contain a sense of inclusion and invitation.

GEESAMAN: That's right. When I see that little picture down there I'm just looking really at the masses, the shapes, the light, and

the color and not paying attention to the details. Because I don't want to see them, and I don't want to print them. Even if they're on the negative, I want to suppress detail.

And you know, there's a flip side to that insecurity. It gives you an edge because it's so terribly important. It gives you a sharpness and a desperation. You have to just make the best of it. It may be raining or cold, or you're getting a cold or anything. But you just have to do it.

KLINKENBORG: You make it sound as if there's a lot of tension. The power of the visual masses that you're seeing must be very strong for them to overcome it.

GEESAMAN: Yes. They have to be strong and my desperation has to be strong too. And then once I see that, all of a sudden all that insecurity and fear doesn't matter anymore because then I just get my attention focused.

I don't know how other people feel. What I'm really doing here is going to an already ordered landscape, and then I'm imposing my own order on it.

So there's an extra tension, I suppose, because I'm not really accepting the landscape for what it is. I'm trying to make it into something and I don't know what that thing is until I see it down there on the screen. But once I see it, I know it's right.

But I don't mean to imply that the anxiety is carried over in the printing. Because that's where I really feel secure.

KLINKENBORG: That's what I was about to ask. It seems to me that the counterpart to this must be what you feel when you're working in your darkroom. It's a place of real enclosure, real security.

GEESAMAN: Right. It is. It's where I feel most centered. And that's where I just take what I've got on the film and try to edit it. And then I try to transform it into something that looks right to me.

Even then I make a lot of 8-by-10-inch prints and put them up on my walls in the basement and think about them, look at them, look at them far away, look at them up close.

I never know how they're going to look in the end. I almost always start by backing away from the predominant color, which is usually green. Let's say, just for example, if you back away from green, then the opposite of that in the darkroom is magenta. I keep taking away green and adding magenta until, oh, it really looks bizarre.

But just at that edge sometimes it takes on a painterly quality because all the color relationships are right.

KLINKENBORG: Keeping that knife edge of clarity and color must be a fascinating prospect in itself.

GEESAMAN: Yes. I never know. I mean I have no rules for myself, which is what I really love about color photography.

KLINKENBORG: Coming out of the deep orthodoxy of black-and-

white, how did you get to a point where there are no rules for yourself?

GEESAMAN: Well, having color is another parameter. And using it, I can't help but push some of the other parameters into the background.

Those other parameters—composition, pattern, structure, symmetry, geometry, verticality—are the ones that always made photography seem so serious to me. And that was why I never would consider doing color. I had an idea that black-and-white was more serious. It had a history and an orthodoxy associated with it. Color seemed a lot less serious to me.

Well, now that's exactly why I like color. Because it seems so freeing.

I think maybe when you've stayed with something for a long time and followed all of its rules and taken it kind of as far as you can, then when another parameter comes along, it's a wonderful surprise.

KLINKENBORG: But I get that feeling that you'd already freed yourself in black-and-white and that color was an enhancement of that liberation.

GEESAMAN: It's interesting that you'd say that. I was at the MacDowell Colony for a few summers, and I just had so much time there, it was overwhelming.

And so I would try to do things I never would do. I'd sit outside my

studio and take some flowers and rub the pollen onto the photograph, use different berries and rub the juice into a photograph. It must have been a sort of intimation of what was going to come. Because I always said I would never do color.

KLINKENBORG: What strikes me about this new work is that in some ways the impact is more immediate. You can read very deeply into these photographs, but they also allow you to get them more quickly if you like.

GEESAMAN: I agree with you. And yet they all have that black-and-white influence.

My own black-and-white work was the influence on it. And it still is, you know. And I don't know if I can ever get away from it.

KLINKENBORG: Your photographs make artificial something that is already intensely artificial, the human landscape, that is.

GEESAMAN: That's exactly what I would say. I would say I'm imposing my own order on an already ordered place. These are really personal appropriations, but they're done with a little bit of arrogance, I suppose. Why would I presume to photograph a tree I don't even know the name of?

KLINKENBORG: Yet these photographs aren't the least bit afraid of beauty.

GEESAMAN: No. I've never felt there was anything wrong with that.

KLINKENBORG: You said something the last time we talked that really struck me. You said that printing color is about finding a unique translation of hidden information in the negative.

GEESAMAN: It's really surprising to me. I never would have known it. It isn't anything I knew would happen, but I discovered it when I printed myself and kept making little adjustments in color and density as I worked.

KLINKENBORG: It gives me an image of you in your studio looking out a giant picture window onto the world and turning the color dials by the side of the window.

GEESAMAN: Oh, that's terribly important. I love that. It just combines everything I love the most about what I do.

LIST OF PHOTOGRAPHS

Editor's note: Included below are the photographer's reference numbers.

Page 54: *Boboli Gardens, Florence, Italy, 2000* (10-00-2c-12)

Page 55: *Monticiano, Tuscany, Italy, 2000* (10-00-6c-9)

Page 56: *Villa Gamberaia, Florence, Italy, 2000* (10-00-16c-12)

Pages 58–59: *Sluis, The Netherlands, 1995* (5-95-33c-8) (detail)

Pages 66–67: *Zemurray Gardens, near Loranger, Louisiana, 2000* (3-00-8c-4) (detail)

Page 69: *Longwood Gardens, Kennett Square, Pennsylvania, 1994* (8-94-4c-2)

Page 70: *Bernheim Arboretum, Clermont, Kentucky, 1993* (5-93-1c-4)

Page 71: *Antietam National Battlefield, Sharpsburg, Maryland, 1996* (4-96-31c-7)

Page 72: *Reflection Riding Arboretum, Chattanooga, Tennessee, 2001* (4-01-30c-4)

Page 73: *Reflection Riding Arboretum, Chattanooga, Tennessee, 2001* (4-01-21c-4)

Page 74: *Hot Springs, Arkansas, 1994* (4-94-1c-6)

Page 76: *Pea Ridge National Military Park, Pea Ridge, Arkansas, 1994* (4-94-14c-12)

Page 77: *Pea Ridge National Military Park, Pea Ridge, Arkansas, 1994* (4-94-14c-7)

Page 78: *Hot Springs, Arkansas 1994* (4-94-1c-3)

Page 79: *Bernheim Arboretum, Clermont, Kentucky, 1999* (10-99-6c-4)

Page 80: *Bernheim Arboretum, Clermont, Kentucky, 1993* (5-93-9c-2)

Page 81: *Cheekwood Gardens, Nashville, Tennessee, 2001* (4-01-26c-9)

Page 82: *Bernheim Arboretum, Clermont, Kentucky, 1994* (10-94-7c-8)

Page 83: *Bernheim Arboretum, Clermont, Kentucky, 1994* (10-94-7c-6)

Page 84: *Bernheim Arboretum, Clermont, Kentucky, 2001* (4-01-28c-1)

Page 85: *Bernheim Arboretum, Clermont, Kentucky, 1999* (10-99-8c-3)

Page 86: *Bernheim Forest, Clermont, Kentucky, 1992* (10-92-6c-1)

Page 87: *Fort Snelling Park, Minneapolis, Minnesota, 1993* (10-93-1c-11)

Page 88: *Mendota Bridge, Minneapolis, Minnesota, 1993* (2-93-5c-11)

Page 89: *Zemurray Gardens, near Loranger, Louisiana, 2000* (3-00-12c-11)

Page 90: *Zemurray Gardens, near Loranger, Louisiana, 2000* (3-00-6c-12)

Page 91: *Live Oak Gardens, near New Iberia, Louisiana, 1993* (3-93-1c-1)

Page 92: *Zemurray Gardens, near Loranger, Louisiana, 2000* (3-00-8c-4)

Page 93: *Avery Island, near Lafayette, Louisiana, 1996* (2-96-11c-1)

Page 94: *Chiricahua National Monument, near Willcox, Arizona, 1994* (2-94-21c-8)

Page 95: *Chiricahua National Monument, near Willcox, Arizona, 1994* (2-94-20c-3)

Page 96: *Filoli Gardens, Woodside, California, 2000* (3-00-31c-1)

Page 97: *Filoli Gardens, Woodside, California, 2000* (3-00-28c-6)

Pages 98–99: *Bernheim Arboretum, Clermont, Kentucky, 2001* (4-01-28c-1) (detail)

Page 100: *Near Tulum, Mexico, 2002* (2-02-6c-5)

Page 101: *Near Tulum, Mexico, 2002* (2-02-6c-2)

Page 102: *Near Tulum, Mexico, 2002* (2-02-16c-7)

ACKNOWLEDGMENTS

I thank Yancey Richardson, who first proposed and encouraged the idea of this book, Janice Stanton of Aperture, and Robert Morton, Aperture's Editor-in-Chief, who made it a reality. I also thank Verlyn Klinkenborg for his insightful essays on my transition to color photography. My appreciation goes to Peter Martin for teaching me how to print in color, JOBO Fototechnic for the technology to do the work myself, and ProColor of Minneapolis for preparing the photographs for publication. For their generous showing of my work over the years, I thank the dealers who have steadfastly supported and encouraged me: Thomas Barry Fine Arts, Minneapolis; Yancey Richardson Gallery, New York; Catherine Edelman Gallery, Chicago; Stephen Cohen Gallery, Los Angeles; Robert Koch Gallery, San Francisco; Jackson Fine Art, Atlanta; Scheinbaum & Russek, Ltd., Santa Fe; Elliott Brown Gallery, Seattle; and Espace Parallèle, Brussels. In particular I wish to emphasize the debt I owe to Thomas Barry, for twenty years of dedicated representation. I am grateful to the Bernheim Forest and Arboretum for their 1991 Artist-in-Residence Fellowship, which led to my first color photographs. For advice and help, I thank my daughters, Rachel Cleveland and Sarah Geesaman. Most of all, however, my gratitude goes to my husband, Donald Geesaman, for his logistical support and intellectual guidance.

Copyright © 2003 Aperture Foundation, Inc.; Photographs copyright © 2003 Lynn Geesaman;
Text copyright © 2003 Verlyn Klinkenborg

All rights reserved under International and Pan-American Copyright Conventions.
No part of this book may be reproduced in any form whatsoever without written permission from the publisher.

Library of Congress Control Number: 2003104873
Hardcover ISBN: 1-931788-20-0

Editor: Robert Morton
Designer: Judith Michael
Production: Lisa A. Farmer, Bryonie Wise

The staff for this book at Aperture Foundation includes:
Ellen S. Harris, Executive Director; Roy Eddey, Director of Finance and Administration; Lisa A. Farmer, Production Director; Robert Morton, Editor-in-Chief, Books; Andrea Smith, Director of Publicity; Linda Stormes, Director of Sales & Marketing; Alan Yamahata, Director of Development; Work-Scholars: Nicola Bodman, Karen Engle, Jeffrey Rogers, Kim Phillips, Annie Wilker, Fran Ula, Gillian Fox

Aperture Foundation, a not-for-profit organization, publishes *Aperture* magazine, books, and limited-edition prints of fine photography and presents photographic exhibitions worldwide. A complete catalog is available on request.

To subscribe to *Aperture* magazine write Aperture, P.O. Box 3000, Denville, New Jersey 07834, or call toll-free: (866) 457-4603. One year: $40.00. Two years: $66.00. International subscriptions: (973) 627-2427. Add $20.00 per year.

Aperture Foundation,
including Book Center and Burden Gallery:
20 East 23rd Street, New York, New York 10010.

Printed in the Czech Republic

First Edition
10 9 8 7 6 5 4 3 2 1

A limited-edition 15-by-15-inch digital c-print from the series *Parc de Sceaux*, 1997, signed and numbered by Lynn Geesaman, is available through Aperture Foundation. The edition is limited to 50 prints and 4 artist's proofs. For more information, visit Aperture's website.

AF807568